PRESERVING *the* PINES

NEW JERSEY *and the* ORIGINS OF ENVIRONMENTALISM

WILLIAM J. LEWIS

Published by The History Press
An imprint of Arcadia Publishing
Charleston, SC
www.historypress.com

Copyright © 2025 by William J. Lewis
All rights reserved

All color photos courtesy of author's collection.

First published 2025

Manufactured in the United States

ISBN 9781467159845

Library of Congress Control Number: 2025933730

Notice: The information in this book is true and complete to the best of our knowledge. It is offered without guarantee on the part of the author or The History Press. The author and The History Press disclaim all liability in connection with the use of this book.

All rights reserved. No part of this book may be reproduced or transmitted in any form whatsoever without prior written permission from the publisher except in the case of brief quotations embodied in critical articles and reviews.

This pile of pages of words and ink is dedicated to people like "Doc" Vivian: teachers, conservationists, tree huggers and all those who care for (all of) the environments in this great galaxy of ours, the Milky Way. The foundation that was built by earlier generations is still there. It started from the tiniest of particles, like the galaxy's planets. Then came the army of environmental groups and, finally, the protection afforded by the New Jersey Pinelands Commission, the New Jersey Department of Environmental Protection (NJDEP) and many others. These folks were field ecologists, historians, environmentalists, naturalists, foresters and, above all else, teachers. To those of you who continue to care even in the face of overwhelming adversity and the plunder of the planet, taking a chapter title from one of Doc's works, written in 1973, "The Unironment—An Uninformed, Uncommitted Society": the mission continues, keep fighting!

CONTENTS

FOREWORD

It was my good fortune to be contacted by author William Joe Lewis regarding his ambitious plan to write a book about the beginnings and progression of a movement to demonstrate interactive methods of learning about the Pine Barrens of New Jersey.

Much of my adult life has been focused on the ecology and culture of the Pinelands Region. Out in the Pine Barrens, it was very special for me to have the guidance and companionship of Dr. V. Eugene Vivian during countless shared adventures, exploring the forests and streams of this unique place. We spent many hours conducting research, working in the field and encountering rare and endangered plants and animals.

Gene taught me and many others how to read the landscape, conduct accurate research and record and interpret our findings. Along the way, he shared excellent methods of hands-on learning, encouraging instructors and their students to experience the environment of the Pine Barrens and to pass on their enthusiasm to friends and classmates.

I do know that this is a well-researched book to read and enjoy, and I feel grateful to have connected with the author, William Joe Lewis.

—Terry O'Leary

ACKNOWLEDGMENTS

I would like to take the time to thank all of you who latch on to historical footnotes, both inside and outside of your homes. Preserving history is a burden we all should happily bear. Speaking of bears, the O'Learys, Cathy and Terry, have been huge in bringing this book to fruition, providing research material and critical guidance. I owe the two of you a huge bear hug. A last-minute bit of crucial information came my way from friend and fellow genealogy researcher Cheryl Moore: thank you for the additional set of hands. To Dr. Vivian's family members (George, Tammy Sue, Nadine, Rae, Doc himself) who have shared family photos, family gatherings and family history, I say thank you, too! Not to mention a heartfelt thank-you to the people who populate historical societies across the United States, especially to president of the Pemberton Township Historic Trust Paulie Wenger and to Sherry Lostaglia Scull, who separately sent me pertinent research material in the nick of time. Lest we forget those who helped narrate these pages by sharing their own stories in personal interviews (Terry, Joe, Mike, Pola, Lillian, Christine, German, Thomas, John, Shaun and James), we salute you, too!

To the advanced readers who lent their expertise and their time to make this book project that much better, I say thank you. Thank you to those keepers of the light, witnesses of history, who remember to pass it on: Janet Larson, Nancy Burke, Shayne Russell and Thomas Besselman. I have great appreciation for your kindness and sharing. The book's walls would not be adorned so well if it wasn't for the fantastic original artwork of acorns, Ms.

Vayda Beck: may you go on to develop your gift and share it with the world! And Taylor Harpster whose artistic talent brought us Preserving the Pines in a canning jar design in the nick of time, a huge thank you! Some of the photos on the walls of this book came to us via an old shoebox of slides thanks to the photographic genius of Dennis McDonald, friend and author extraordinaire. While on special assignment, Mr. McDonald happily and most expertly shot the village of Whitesbog as it is today. In my opinion, his wife, Rose McDonald, takes shots just as good, if not better. I thank her for the contribution to the project. To the thousands of fans who make up the online and offline community of Piney Tribe, as always, you know: I appreciate you, too!

INTRODUCTION

> *Any writer of History needs to admit that it is manufactured, brewed in the mind of the historian who brings to his work much in the way of bias. The historian then makes history and chooses the persons, places, and things that he wishes to be deified and memorialized. In addition, the historian is too often the victim of his own indoctrination, prejudice, and value systems, hence any attempt at objectivity seems fated to fail, for the historian plays judge and jury, choosing those historical facts and persons he deems as important and sentencing, as it were, the others to historical oblivion.*
>
> —*Robert W. Harper*

It's with the sentiment from the quote of Robert W. Harper that we delve into the history of a place that is well documented, the birthplace of the modern-day blueberry (first sold in 1916 under the name Tru-Blue-Berries). We will do our best not to fall prey to the folly of self-prejudice, the rewriting of history and patriarchal worship. A period of history has been forgotten when it shouldn't have been, but we'll soon find out what and where that was and who was the mighty oak that planted the seed(s). The seeds were acorns, and the wave of saplings spread across the region and the state. Why should you care? History paints a picture of the same recurring theme: one by one, those who care teach the next generation to care. Seeds of hope and acorns grow to become mighty oak trees. The kindness of the human spirit is recycled and rekindled, repeatedly.

Cranberry picking at Whitesbog Village, predating the 1960s. *From the Whitesbog, New Jersey Photograph Collection at the Burlington County Library, Westampton, New Jersey.*

Predating the crossbreeding of wild huckleberry bushes by famed heroine Elizabeth Coleman White and USDA agent Fredrick Coville was the work of Elizabeth's father, Joseph J. White, an accomplished cranberry farmer, whose book *Cranberry Culture: A Practical Grower* was published in 1870. The book documented how to succeed as a cranberry farmer while solidifying White in the history books as someone who succeeded in cultivating wild cranberries. J.J. White built the village of Whitesbog, named after him, to house his budding cranberry operation and ensure his place in the history of the cranberry.

Each of the village buildings at Whitesbog over the years has served multiple purposes. In both J.J. White and Elizabeth's lifetimes, the physical buildings made of wood served to propagate the production of cranberries and, later, blueberries. Most but not all of Whitesbog Village, which was built guided by their astute leadership and entrepreneurial spirit, has survived today. Like humankind's own bodies and minds, many things of old drift into memory, forgotten and torn down by the weathering of time. Today, Whitesbog closely resembles a ghost town found in the Pine Barrens of southern New Jersey. Adding to the many forgotten towns of the Pines, its boards and cement foundations have become relics of lives from past generations. The creations of man in the farming industry fell into disrepair through neglect and the absence of grandiose ideas along with a work ethic to make those ideas become reality.

Cranberry packing facility at Whitesbog Village, predating the 1960s. *From the Whitesbog, New Jersey Photograph Collection at the Burlington County Library, Westampton, New Jersey.*

Whitesbog Village aerial circa early 1960s. *From the Whitesbog, New Jersey Photograph Collection at the Burlington County Library, Westampton, New Jersey.*

Eventually, a rallying call could be heard to save and preserve Whitesbog Village by way of state preservation efforts. In 1961, a mechanism was put in place to aid the fight to preserve dwindling stores of open space in New Jersey. Environmentalism was beginning to blossom in the state. Overdevelopment was both a statewide and a national problem. The New Jersey Department of Environmental Protection, born the same day as the first-ever Earth Day, in April 1970, utilized citizen-approved legislation founding and funding land preservation efforts called the Green Acres Bond Act (1961). Both in New Jersey and, more broadly, across the United States, society collectively began to place a high value on land preservation to combat urban sprawl and providing local community parks to give all citizens access to outdoor recreation. This is part of the hidden history of J.J. White's village, one yet to be written down and recovered, as we will discover within these pages.

Preserving the Pines design by Taylor Harpster. *Author's collection.*

An African proverb describes the No. 1 reason for the existence of a village of people: "It takes a village to raise a child." Raising a child and educating a child (in this case, many children) are part of the hidden history of Whitesbog Village, as we will soon find out. Who will be there when the generations of people who fought for a local village like Whitesbog to be preserved try to pass the mantle of environmental stewardship on; who will receive it? Why, the child of tomorrow, of course—we hope, with great faith! Abstractly, we know the "village" as a community space is important, but how do we impress upon the next generation its importance? What dollar value do we assign to environmental education (EE)? "Save the Earth"—for who? You and I are dust in the wind, yet the child remains. So we hope, with great faith, that the fight will go on.

In 1966, a new leader emerged to take the reins of a place now part of the state Green Acres program. From 1966 to 1984, a professor from Glassboro State College (now Rowan University), Dr. V. Eugene Vivian, with a grandiose idea and purpose, set forth to educate and instill empathy for "all environments" in tens of thousands of students, children and adults. There,

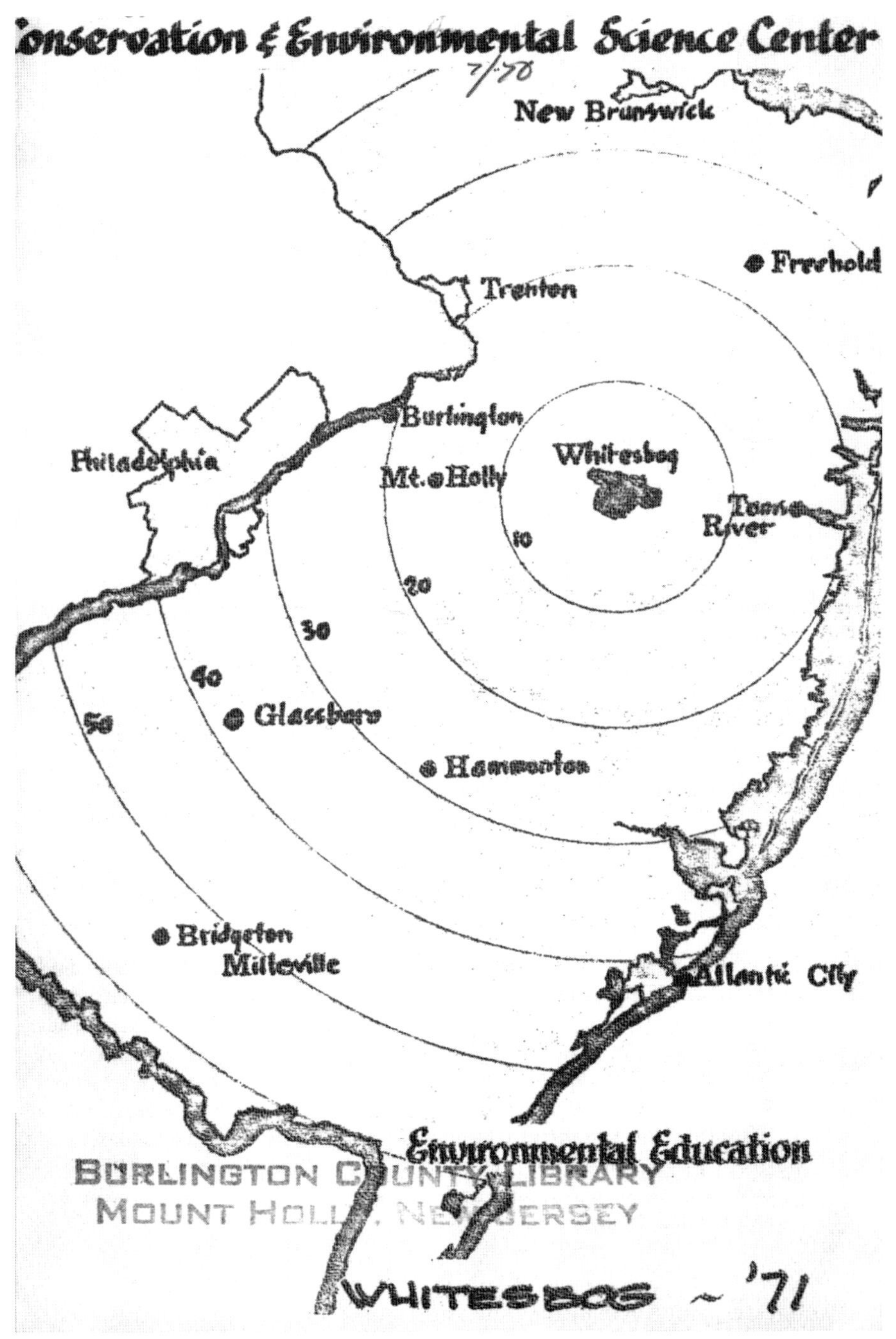

Pamphlet advertising the services of the newly established Conservation and Environmental Science Center (CESC) in 1971. *Courtesy Burlington County Library*.

in the vicinity of Browns Mills, New Jersey, stood a berry farmstead—both cranberries and blueberries—in the village known as Whitesbog.

This is the story of the in-between years: in between the history of yesterday, today and the rapid advance of the future. In industry, business-minded people see a guiding hand or an invisible hand, per Adam Smith, who wrote in 1776 of an invisible hand at work in free markets, ensuring all humanity receives needed resources. Another invisible hand is at play in another human endeavor—or maybe not so invisible to those who focus on the environmental heroes and heroines of the past century and today. People from all walks of life are united to carry the torch or baton of environmental education and good stewardship.

We have great faith and hope for the future by one means. That means to an end is a selfless act: teaching. It's even more than being selfless. Great teachers all have one thing in common: they lack the typical ego-driven mindset. How can one have an ego when one will not see 90 percent of the seeds they plant grow? The world needs more professional educators and nonformal teachers who share their knowledge gained through years of experience. And as a society, we need to do better at shining a light on the people who do good. All too often, the villain is remembered. Must everyone know the name Hitler and what he did? But name a man or a woman who fought against his tyranny. Let us continue to shine light on the good of humanity. If the doers of good get caught up in a movement, then someone should write a book about it.

Come with me to learn about the history of the Conservation and Environmental Studies Center (1966–84) in Whitesbog Village and about the man who was known among his peers as a mighty oak in the field of environmental education, Professor Emeritus Dr. V. Eugene Vivian. He was at the center of Whitesbog Village, creating and leading the charge that echoed the African proverb adapted to his cause: "It takes a village of teachers to raise and educate a child." In this case, the efforts of many villages and villagers came together, a collective or hive of learned behavior and respect, to value the importance of the 1.1 million acres of woods that would ultimately become the New Jersey Pinelands National Reserve. Educators like Dr. Vivian led us to preserve the Pines in the first place, illustrating that *environmentalism* isn't a bad word. It wasn't just one person with a pen but many with heartfelt feelings toward the environment and a commitment to our shared history. Integral to our journey are the acorns turned into oak trees and the nests or nurseries that harbored and ushered our greatest assets into the unknown tomorrow. Each has a direct connection to Dr. Vivian, with his sixty-five years of teaching experience, and is also connected through "Doc" and the environmental educator web of New Jersey.

> *Of all that there is on earth, nothing is taken away by life and nothing is added by life—but nearly everything is used by life, used and reused in thousands of complex ways, moved through vast chains of plants and animals and back again to the beginning. Any break in these chains can spoil the whole. The web of life has so many threads that a few can be broken without making it all unravel (and if this were not so, life could not have survived the normal accidents of weather and time), but still, the snapping of each thread makes the whole web shudder, and weakens it.*
>
> —*From* The Stockholm Conference: Only One Earth *(1972)*

Chapter 1

THE HUMBLE BEGINNINGS OF VINCENT EUGENE VIVIAN

True or False Question

The strongest oak tree of the forest is not the one that is protected from the storm and hidden from the sun. It's the one that stands in the open where it is compelled to struggle for its existence against the winds and rains and the scorching sun.

—*Napoleon Hill*

In 1946, Dr. Harley P. Milstead, professor of geography at State Teachers College in Montclair, New Jersey, wrote *New Jersey People, Resources, and Industries of the Garden State*, a guide for teachers educating young minds about various aspects of their home state. In the "Gazetteer" section, he listed cities of New Jersey with ten thousand or more citizens. Milstead painted a picture of a town that was significant in forming one of the country's top pioneers in the environmental education movement. Paterson, full of remnant nineteenth-century manufacturing industries, seemed like an unlikely place for an environmental sprout to spring from. "Paterson is a city of great industrial diversification," Milstead wrote, "with the metal trades, textiles, furniture, woven labels, chemicals, and mirrors taking the leading roles." But it was there, in postindustrial Paterson, New Jersey, that Dr. V. Eugene Vivian was schooled.

Dr. Vivian with a favorite fedora hat on; in the background, the cranberry bogs of Whitesbog. *Photo credit Dan Katz.*

Known as "Doc" to both friends and family, Vincent Eugene Vivian was born on May 12, 1915, to two loving parents in Paterson, New Jersey, in Passaic County. His Italian-born, naturalized father, Salvatore (1884–1969), was the owner-operator of a women's clothing store, and his mother was New Jersey native Isabel Vivian, née Steinberg (1891–1975). Loving new mother Isabel, who was listed in the 1920 federal census as vice president of the family clothing store, brought Eugene home to the couple's tiny apartment on Graham Avenue in Paterson. Before he turned five, the family moved six blocks to attain a larger residence on Park Avenue in Paterson, New Jersey. It wasn't much of a change in scenery: another bustling city street corner on which the children weren't allowed to ride their bikes because of the danger traffic posed. Eugene and his little brother, Donald Robert (born in 1926), spent their formative years in the city region of Paterson, New Jersey. Their maternal grandmother, Vera Steinberg, lived with the family there.

Fast-forward to age fourteen (1929–30): young Vivian was actively working toward the twenty-one merit badges required to earn the coveted status of Eagle Scout after becoming a Life Scout. He prided himself on receiving a merit badge for botany:

> *Encouraged by my mother, I was very interested in the special awards in camp (Camp Alhtaha at Awosting on Greenwood Lake) for identifying 300 plants and was awarded the "Oak Leaf" when I succeeded. There were not many*

> *"Oak Leafs" among the Boy Scouts. Then I went on to identify a total of 500 plants for which I received the "Acorn" award, and through the wisdom of Chief Lottee, pledged to produce other "Acorns" and train two other Scouts.*

In his adolescence, finding his way on the trail of life, Doc went to public school at Eastside High School in Paterson. Eastside High School, founded in 1926, was still sparkling clean and full of knowledge, and young Eugene's parents had great expectations and dreams for the boy's future. He graduated in 1932. A slight rift of sorts occurred between Eugene and his parents. His Italian father and German mother lived the American dream, using their own ability and elbow grease to build something for the next generation. Doc's father would often, in a kind way, pick on Doc for wanting to be an Eagle Scout, and he didn't quite understand the fascination or infatuation his young son had with the out-of-doors. Salvatore was a firm guiding hand in his life, and like every young boy, Eugene often sought his father's approval.

After receiving his Acorn award, young Eugene worked as a nature counselor at Camp Alhtaha for two summers. One of the responsibilities of a nature counselor was to teach the younger scouts how to identify twenty-five plant species so they could earn points to get the much-coveted Camp Alhtaha insignia. Life lessons are learned best from a trusted source. These are the lessons that stick with you the longest and the best. Young Eugene's father observed an interaction between his son and other young campers at Alhtaha and, in his quiet way, revealed what he saw to his budding naturalist,

> *You are a terrible nature counselor. I would not ask you anything! I asked him why and he said, "You are not clear in your instruction; not interesting to talk to because you act so high and mighty!" Eugene Vivian recalls, "It*

V. EUGENE VIVIAN

It is fitting that this exponent of the great out-doors should be a physicist. The historic memory of his plaids, his goatee and his diary throw a legendary glow on his policy of never-a-dull-moment. He's ambitious, he's amusing, he's stubborn. He never would account for that first "V".

High school yearbook photo of young V. Eugene Vivian. *Author's collection.*

was a very important lesson for me because I so much wanted my father's approval. As a result, I learned to speak encouragingly and volunteer much information. I "turned on" to my campers, not "off."

The story was recorded by Rae Walton in her self-published 2003 book, *The Ancestry of Vincent Eugene Vivian*.

This was a great life lesson learned from a trusted source—even for an overachieving Acorn award recipient at the ripe old age of fifteen. In many families where parents own and operate a business, their dream is for a better future for their children. Eugene's parents expected that the children would take over the family business. Neither Doc nor his younger brother, Donald Robert (Doc was ten years his senior), cared to carry on the torch for the family business in cloth manufacturing. Salvatore immigrated to the United States in 1910, in a period when Italian immigrants were looked on as undesirable or far worse by those who felt their factory jobs were threatened by the cheap labor of newly arrived immigrants. Records show Mr. Vivian was once Mr. Viviano, who immigrated from Polizzi Generosa, in the province of Palermo on the island of Sicily in southern Italy. The racial disparities immigrants experienced in America ran rampant and could be enough of an incentive to change one's name and mannerisms just to fit in. Just having a factory job was enough for Salvatore, who dropped the *o* in the family surname, Viviano. Yet he had greater hopes for his children's future and supported them taking on higher education, even if it meant not following in the family business—thus helping plant the seed of the future environmental education movement.

On that path, Doc took with him what he learned as an Acorn, a philosophy he carried with him throughout his life and a responsibility he took seriously to teach the next generation: "An acorn becomes an oak tree." In the United States, rugged individualism conflicts with the societal consciousness. Doc discovered early on in his studies that Napoleon Hill's quote, when posed as a true or false question, wasn't an easy one to answer. Being a lone oak tree could be ruinous to an education movement and, in general, to one's life. There in the landscape, for all to see, is the lone mighty oak. It stands tall, firmly anchored to the landscape but destined to fall. It would rather be amid other trees than stand alone, sharing the struggles of weathering storms and the elements together. As he witnessed the Boy Scouts organization recruit and train soon-to-be scouts, Doc understood what it meant to be an Acorn—more than just earning a Pioneer merit badge or an Oak Leaf or an Acorn award.

Boy Scouts of America pamphlet circa 1936. *Courtesy Scout Patch Auction.*

In Doc's own words, "That kind of responsibility of reproducing yourself always stayed with me," as reported in the *Press of Atlantic City* by staff writer Michael McGarry in 1991. One scout could survive, but a troop of scouts could accomplish so much more.

Years later, in 1937, when he was in his early twenties, Doc served as assistant camp director, Alhtaha Council, Boy Scouts of America. In the same timeframe, he graduated from Montclair State College of New Jersey (1936) and taught all the sciences—general science, chemistry, biology and physics—at a high school in Park Ridge, New Jersey (1936–39). Eventually, he returned to his own alma mater, Eastside High in Paterson, from 1939

Dr. V. Eugene Vivian's first teaching job in physics class at Park Ridge High School, New Jersey, 1938. *Courtesy Nadine & George Young.*

New address

SERIAL NUMBER: 2282 | 1. NAME (Print): VINCENT (First) EUGENE (Middle) VIVIAN (Last) | ORDER NUMBER: 2304

2. ADDRESS (Print): 190 CARROLL STREET (Number and street or R. F. D. number) PATERSON (Town) PASSAIC (County) N.J. (State)

3. TELEPHONE: NONE; LA-3-7554 (Exchange) (Number)

4. AGE IN YEARS: 25; DATE OF BIRTH: 5/12/15 (Mo.) (Day) (Yr.)

5. PLACE OF BIRTH: Paterson (Town or county) NEW JERSEY (State or country)

6. COUNTRY OF CITIZENSHIP: U.S.A.

7. NAME OF PERSON WHO WILL ALWAYS KNOW YOUR ADDRESS: MRS. (Mr., Mrs., Miss) BETTY (First) ELDER (Middle) VIVIAN (Last)

8. RELATIONSHIP OF THAT PERSON: WIFE

9. ADDRESS OF THAT PERSON: 190 CARROLL STREET (Number and street or R. F. D. number) PATERSON (Town) PASSAIC (County) NEW JERSEY (State)

10. EMPLOYER'S NAME: BOARD OF EDUCATION

11. PLACE OF EMPLOYMENT OR BUSINESS: CITY HALL (Number and street or R. F. D. number) PATERSON (Town) PASSAIC (County) N.J. (State)

I AFFIRM THAT I HAVE VERIFIED ABOVE ANSWERS AND THAT THEY ARE TRUE.

REGISTRATION CARD
D. S. S. Form 1
(over)

V. Eugene Vivian
(Registrant's signature)

Dr. Eugene Vivian's World War II draft card. *Author's collection.*

to 1945. A bit of movie trivia for the reader: in the 1989 film *Lean on Me*, starring Morgan Freeman, another East High School educator/principal, Joe Louis Clark, gains fame for his tough approach to keeping kids in school.

On his World War II draft card, we get a glimpse of Doc's stature at the age of twenty-five: he had well-kept brown hair and rich dark brown eyes, stood five foot nine and weighed in at 140 pounds. At this period in his life, he was a newly married husband. He met his first wife, Elizabeth "Betty" Vivian, née Elder, at Montclair State Teachers College; the college sweethearts were married on August 28, 1940. They had two children, Mark Vivian and Joan Freeman, née Vivian. Unfortunately, an amicable divorce was on the horizon for the two teachers, who split in 1955.

Something fortuitous happened to Doc after he got hired by Paterson State College to teach two courses in chemistry—maybe not so much by accident, as Eugene Vivian was making a name for himself, and he had many mighty oaks as mentors who invited the acorn to crown with the rest of the oaks. He had, just a few years prior, in 1940, received his master's degree in botany from Columbia University.

> *At Paterson, I also had a new experience in my life, which was working at National Camp directed by Dr. Lloyd B. Sharp who envisioned National Camp as a place to develop courses and opportunities for people to do research work in outdoor education. Lloyd Sharp had written a doctoral thesis in 1928 demonstrating how outdoor education provided an atmosphere and environment where learning could take place better than limited to just the classroom. I was very much attracted to this because I had always been much interested in having direct "hands-on" experiences for students of all ages, especially when I would take college classes outdoors to see first-hand what we talked about in the classroom.**

It was at National Camp and, later, the New Jersey School of Conservation (SOC) where Doc surely encountered another legend in the outdoor education movement alongside Dr. L.B. Sharp—a peer of Sharp's and a person Sharp leaned on during the early years at National Camp until he and his wife left for other adventures in 1945. Author Julie Carson writes,

> *From 1939 until 1945,* [William Vinal] *taught at National Camp as the primary naturalist. Captain Bill, who was a professor of nature education at the University of Massachusetts in Amherst, developed a*

* From *The Ancestry of Vincent Eugene Vivian* (self-published, 2003).

> *Socratic method of teaching in the outdoors. The Socratic method was not giving the answer but instead asking penetrating questions, leading questions, where the learner begins to lean on his or her own by hands-on type of sensitivity, gathering the facts through the senses. He was a master teacher.*

Carson is quoting a 2001 interview with Dr. Rillo, an environmental education teacher and contemporary of Dr. Vivian, in her 2009 book *Never Finished…Just Begun*. Professor Vinal's technique was no secret, for he had published several widely distributed books, one of them being *Nature Recreation: Group Guidance for the Out-of-Doors* (first published in 1940 and then again in 1963 by Dover). Two quotes stick out from *Nature Recreation*, which would have been in Dr. Vivian's massive environmental education library collection, and are great food for thought:

> *It is the old trail law of stop, look, and listen. If you stop, you may learn. If you look, you may see. If you listen, you may hear.*

> *He has been ingrained with a pedagogy that says that the way we think about these facts is much more important than the facts themselves.*

In 1955, Doc, with his second wife, Norma T. Vivian, packed up and left Paterson State College, moving to Glassboro State College, bringing with him the outdoor environmental educational movement. He was also influenced by his experiences with the old guard of out-of-doors education, creating something of a mesh of old and new in his approach to teaching as part of the budding environmental education movement. In July 2007, during a founder's group of the New Jersey School of Conservation (SOC) interview with Annette Sambolin, Doc described the outlook he gained from his experience at SOC and the movement's direction in his eyes:

> *The idea of students and teachers learning in the out-of-doors is part of environmental ed. Environmental ed has outdoor ed content, and that content is really a methodology. How do you teach about the environment? And the idea is to experience it yourself. And then you can transmit that with experiences and words to any person whom you are taking outdoors to learn anything they desire. So it's the idea of hands-on experiences having the greatest persistence of learning.*

Above: Dr. Vivian with hand lens inspecting Franklin tree (*Franklinia alatamaha*) at the General Store, Whitesbog Village, Browns Mills, New Jersey.

Right: Dr. Vivian with hand lens inspecting Franklin tree (*Franklinia alatamaha*) at the General Store, Whitesbog Village, Browns Mills, New Jersey. *September 7, 1975* Trenton Times *press photo by Calvin Solliday*.

But the idea of bringing students and teachers together to teach the youngsters to find themselves using the methods of direct experience for environmental education. I can only use Glassboro State as an example. I made it my responsibility to have people in each of the departments, whether it was education, history, or sciences, of course, for ways in which the different disciplines of the college could use environmental or outdoor education methodologies in getting/providing much more effective instrumentation.

During his time at Glassboro, Gene received his doctorate from New York University, in 1958. He also authored or coauthored two different pieces of federal legislation that dovetailed with his EE teaching intentions. The first breathed life into the state School of Conservation (SOC); the second was what he had dreamed of since his first experience with L.B. Sharp at National Camp.

Gene and Dr. Edward J. Ambry together wrote the federal legislative proposal of the 1967–68 school year "for the Experienced Teacher Fellowship for SOC that was submitted to the U.S. Office of Education." Basically, it would "require all teacher preparation students at the six state colleges to attend outdoor leadership training." This successfully positioned the SOC to receive a three-year federal grant issued under Title V of the Elementary and Secondary Education Act (ESA) of the United States, "during President Lyndon B. Johnson's term. Johnson's goal was to initiate the program with expectations that local cooperating funding agencies would continue it after the three-year federal grant expired." Receiving that grant was a wonderful boost to the team in charge of creating Camp Wapalanne at the New Jersey School of Conservation, which still exists some seventy-five years later. The following excerpt is from the original brochure. You can feel the excitement and energy in those who were making the offer and imagine that of those who would be taking part.

The program provides basic courses in outdoor education and conservation and allows students to select related courses in several departments (outdoor education and conservation, environmental science, social sciences, professional education, and behavioral sciences). By cutting across departmental lines, individual programs may be designed for students which will strengthen their academic background and also allow them to be introduced to new fields of study which will relate to their plans to conduct education programs in outdoor situations.

The Little Folks Need Folklore

FOLKLORE BUFFS in South Jersey know about how the Jersey Devil has been giving Joe Mulliner and the Swamp Angels and many other legitimate South Jersey folklore figures a bad deal.

He is giving them a bad deal because the Jersey Devil, who some people claim stands seven feet tall and glows in the dark in a very ugly way, gets all the publicity even though record has it that no one has ever shook his hand or spoken with him.

While people write about this mythical character, legitimate folklore figures prominent in the history of South Jersey are remaining virtually unknown.

Norma T. Vivian knows about this and she understands. Norma T. Vivian reads every old book she can find to glean and record South Jersey folklore.

Mrs. Vivian, who lives in a house in the heart of the Pine Barrens with her husband Eugene — who is a faculty member at Glassboro State — says that legitimate South Jersey folklore should be taught to our children because folklore preserves the local personality of an area.

Today Norma T. Vivian works to preserve South Jersey in at least two ways. By day she works editing educational material on environment preservation for the South Jersey Conservation and Environment Science Center, in Browns Mills.

FOR MUCH of her spare time, however, Mrs. Vivian collects folklore about South Jersey and tries to pass it along to children and their teachers.

The stories have survived the ravages of time. Some are still just stories told by a fireplace or over coffee. Many have been recorded. All of them are called folklore and they figure very heavily in the important history of South Jersey.

"Preserving folklore preserves the local color of a section," Norma T. Vivian will tell you. "Teach some to your kids and get them interested." She says she tries.

People might like to talk about the Jersey Devil, Mrs. Vivian explains, but few know about the Swamp Angels.

"These Swamp Angels, unlike the Jersey Devil, shook hands and spoke with many people during the days of the Revolutionary War," she will say.

Article on Norma T. Vivian in the *Courier-Post*, January 25, 1971. *Credit Monday with Mike Wolk.*

By another stroke of genius and a stroke of the pen, Dr. Vivian would find and continue to expand the concept of environmental education in a forgotten town in South Jersey for all South Jersey children. More on that in chapter 4, "Beyond Four Walls"—the title being a homage to Dr. Vivian's mentor and friend Dr. L.B. Sharp.

Dr. V. Eugene Vivian was a practicing Christian, as was most of the Vivian family, who spent the years 1930 to 1975 with the community contained within the four walls of East Side Presbyterian Church in Paterson. Before the family moved to this church—at the urging of young Eugene, who was looking to join Boy Scout Troop 3 in Paterson—baby Eugene was baptized in 1934 at the Episcopal church in Paterson. Later in life, on January 7, 1962, he was confirmed, after moving to Pitman, New Jersey, and joining the congregation at the Church of the Good Shepherd. Both he and his second wife, Norma, were confirmed on the same day. Norma Torrents Vivian (1924–1972) was born in New York City. In December 1943, when she was in her mid-twenties, she married her first husband, Wilson N. Pratt, in New York City. She died at the age of forty-seven while living in Whitesbog Village and married to Doc Vivian. Theirs was a second marriage for both of them. Between the two of them, they had two sons, Carlos W. and Mark E., and three daughters, Mrs. Joan Molino, Mrs. Tracy Shisler and the youngest, Norma Gene, named after both her parents, Eugene and Norma.

Norma T. Vivian became a correspondent for numerous regional papers, including the *Woodbury Times* (now the *Gloucester County Times*), the *Philadelphia Evening Bulletin*, the *Inquirer* and the *Camden Courier Post*. Both the *Bulletin* and the *Inquirer* were delivered to homes in the afternoon back then, as they were both relatively cheap for families who subscribed to both. It's said Norma took over a *Camden Courier-Post* column once written by the legendary folklorist and author of *Forgotten Towns and Pine Barrens*, Henry Charlton Beck. A Pine Barrens folklorist herself, she wrote and published a 1965 book titled *Tours Through Historic West Jersey*, presenting to groups like the Woman's Club of Vineland—a true champion of keeping local and state folklore in the minds of young children. She was also an accomplished writer for the *Inquirer* from 1967 to 1969, as well as serving as the PR director for her husband's Conservation & Environmental Studies Center. Like many women then and today, she established a career to support the blended family's budget, and she juggled being a mother of five and the wife of a mighty oak. She threw her weight into supporting her husband's grand aspirations, and as you'll see, she was Dr. Vivian's grandest and most effective champion.

Those years at Glassboro State College from 1955 to 1979, when Doc was chairman of the Science Department and/or a professor there, were formative years for his philosophy on teaching and environmental education. Glassboro's yearbook was called the *Oak*. Was it a coincidence that the symbology of the acorn, representing what would be, and the oak tree, which continues the cycle by producing more acorns, seemingly followed and met up with Doc wherever he went? In the *Oak* yearbook of 1960, the caption accompanying an image of Doc (with his bowtie on and wearing a suit) reads, "The Science Department provides students with the basic foundations in the physical and biological sciences which are necessary for intelligent citizenship in the world today. The department will expand its facilities and offerings next year to provide more specialized training for students who wish to major in Science."

Glassboro State College *Oak* yearbook, 1960. *Author's collection.*

Science

The Science Department provides students with the basic foundations in the physical and biological sciences which are necessary for intelligent citizenship in the world today. The department will expand its facilities and offerings next year to provide more specialized training for students who wish to major in Science.

Dr. V. Eugene Vivian
Chairman

Dr. Vivian, pictured in the 1960 Glassboro State College *Oak* yearbook. *Author's collection.*

Professor Dr. V. Eugene Vivian fostered an environment that sparked debate, inviting diversity of thought while reinforcing traditional science-based knowledge.

A prime example of this is when Doc invited to one of his Glassboro State College classes a fringe Russian American psychoanalyst and author, Immanuel Velikovsky. In an interview, Thomas Gallia, vice president emeritus of Rowan University, had an interesting story to tell about this event that unfolded back when he was a student of Dr. Vivian's. Listen to him explain the teaching mastery of Dr. Vivian and of his college encounter with Velikovsky:

> *Immanuel Velikovsky was the man who wrote the book* Worlds in Collision*—several books to his credit. One of the things Gene did was he brought people in that were on the fringes of things and allowed those people to speak to the students, and we as students learned science wasn't as clean, neat and ordinal as we were led to believe. Velikovsky made incredible predictions. Gene invited this bestselling writer, Immanuel Velikovsky, to talk to the science majors about his radical ideas. He was a very rough*

and intimidating man, in his appearance and his demeanor. Gene had the students write questions on note cards. Mr. Velikovsky destroyed the few students' questions that stood in front of the class and asked him. Dr. Vivian asked me to ask my question. Being intimidated after seeing what the other students went through, I asked my question and was surprised it was well received by Mr. Velikovsky.

In 1966–67, after class was over, the other students and I were shaking our heads like this guy was from another world. Doc invited me over for dinner as Immanuel Velikovsky was coming over for dinner too. When I got there, Gene asked me if I was twenty-one, which I said I was, and he said, "Good, you can have a bit of bourbon." And Velikovsky liked the bourbon. Through the night, they were talking, and the subject came around to Russian folk songs. So Gene brought out his accordion and started playing these songs, and Velikovsky started singing them. Picture it: we were sitting on Gene's front porch in Pitman singing these Russian folk songs, drinking bourbon accompanied by accordion music that then evolved into Italian folk songs.

Then Gene handed me the accordion, saying, "You can play the accordion; you're a good Italian boy." I said, "Yes, I can." I played and he sang "O Sole Mio" ["My Sunshine," a Neapolitan folk song] *and we had such a blast. But it must have been a real scene. An experience I'll never forget. Here was this man that we all revered and feared, Immanuel Velikovsky, who had another side to him: a folksy side, a gregarious side, a "humble person of the people" kind of side. And we enjoyed each other's company. And Gene brought that out. Gene wasn't afraid of it. Some scientists would not want to be associated with any of that stuff. Gene wanted his students to be open-minded about stuff that came in from all kinds of sources and to challenge it and give it as much or as little respect as it was due based on what seemed to be true. He could put things in proper perspective. You don't laugh at them, you don't mock them. You give them a chance to speak, and you say, "Well, I believe it," or "I don't believe it," but in any event, you give the person time to air their ideas. And we should be discussing these things.*

Chapter 2

A NATIONWIDE ENVIRONMENTAL MOVEMENT STIRS

Outdoor Education Supplanted by Environmental Education?

Nature-study is for everyone, and therefore is fundamental; scientific investigation is for the few, and therefore special. If nature-study opens the sympathies natureward, it will increase the appreciation for science.

Nature-study is not science. It is not knowledge. It is not facts. It is spirit. It is concerned with the child's outlook on the world.

Every person's view is necessarily colored by his own field of observation.

We speak of bad weather, as if weather ever could be bad. Weather is not a human institution, and is not to be measured by human standards. There is strength and mighty uplift in the roaring winds that go roistering over the winter hills. The cold and the storm are part of winter, as the warmth and the soft rain are a part of summer. Persons who find happiness in the out-of-doors only in what we call pleasant weather, do not really love nature.

—*Excerpts from Liberty Hyde Bailey's monumental 1903 book* The Nature-Study Idea

Before the 1960s "peace and love" movement, the United States had been through several revolts of thought. At the beginning of the twentieth century, studying nature was a tool for teachers to combat the fatigue families felt brought on by the Industrial Revolution. The distribution of

Americans shifted from rural countryside to urban cities. In the 1940s, those same families who remembered fondly the United States they grew up in wanted their children to experience nature as they did. Camping programs were developed and reinvented by church programs and, eventually, school programs both on-site and off campus.

Today, in the twenty-first century, in the public forum we debate the merits of science. Back then, it was nature versus science, too—not a fight but a discussion about how far to take science teaching to the youth of America. L.H. Bailey was one of the mighty oak leaders of the period, who, before writing the book *The Nature-Study Idea*, wrote the first environmental education teacher handout. "The first leaflet written by Bailey was titled 'How a Squash Plant Gets Out of Its Seed.' Some of the early titles written by Bailey were: 'A Plant at School,' 'How Trees Look in Winter,' 'Four Apple Twigs,' 'A Children's Garden,' 'How Plants Live Together,' 'The Birds and I,' and 'Planting a Plant.'" The teaching of nature continued and evolved in the classroom, supporting a once agrarian society.

It wasn't until the 1940s that a delineator became apparent in the outdoor and environmental education movement. One root of the tree of environmental education was wilderness camping, and another root was teaching in the classroom—with varying shades of green in between. Note that it's described as a delineator and not a crack. Teachers using the same curriculum designed to be used in the classroom and the field had different ends in mind. One root of the oak tree took them one way, whereas the other root of the same tree took others another way. The foundation or roots for many had the same empathic environmental academic heroes and heroines teaching toward the same end, who taught philosophy, environmental education and pedagogy to save the Earth for everyone.

At one end of the outdoor and environmental education spectrum was author and professor Dr. Thomas J. Rillo, who attended Panzer College, which specialized in physical education, and at the other end was Dr. V. Eugene Vivian, future star of environmental education in New Jersey. Both with Italian immigrant fathers, both born and bred North Jerseyans, they were just two of the many emerging environmental education leaders of the time. In Dr. Rillo's book *Historical and Philosophical Foundations of Outdoor and Environmental Education*, he describes one of his mentors in primitive wilderness camping or group camping, which was a big part of outdoor education: "Dr. Lloyd B. Sharp experimented very early with church camping. At National Camp, a training center for outdoor leaders during the 1940s through early sixties, Sharp conducted six-week institutes for church camping leaders and their camp personnel. Sharp worked with the United Methodist Church and the United Church of Christ initially and later included other denominations."

Dr. L.B. Sharp was a man whom Dr. Vivian would quote often throughout his career in environmental education (EE). Vivian echoes the teaching of L.B. Sharp: "Outdoor ed meant teaching best in the out-of-doors what could be best taught there." EE in its current form harks back to this delineation between the two factions. Yet they are blended in such a way that, depending on the purpose and the setting, some can't distinguish the two. And in other cases, EE has become too scientific, which L.H. Bailey warned of in 1903. In his book, Dr. Rillo quotes L.B. Sharp talking about the proverbial writing on the wall for public camping. Sharp saw the differences and the changes yet to come, which were rekindled after World War II, in 1946, and a new need:

> *There is a growing recognition across the country that conservation education is vital to the future economy of this nation. It is becoming more obvious, too, that real conservation can only be taught by bringing students into direct contact with the problems involved. This, of course, means outdoor education and camping education. But before there can be a very widespread or successful move in this direction it will be necessary to train teachers in the techniques of outdoor education. There is some evidence that this type of training is now being offered to teachers and prospective teachers in a variety of ways.*

Sharp was influenced by the previous generation of educators, like John Dewey, while at Teacher's College at Columbia University. Julie Carlson, in her book dedicated to the life of L.B. Sharp, quotes an interview with Dr. Rillo, in which he stated, "The 'New Educators' themselves were a vanguard of a new approach to emphasizing the community in education, using the community as a laboratory, going beyond the four walls of the classroom."

Many saw what could be done in an outdoor setting at the time and how it complemented the different learning styles of students. In some cases, out-of-door classrooms were the best place to teach a subject—not just science but also humanities, English literature, math and so on. These traditional schoolroom classes could be taught in an outdoor setting by a trained professional teacher. The child would retain more by seeing what was at hand and being familiar with their environment. Dr. Vivian, in an interview, once said, "We have evidence that students learn better and more permanently when they are taking part in these environmental and outdoor education experiences…compared to traditional learning."

A New Jersey statewide cumulation of outdoor and environmental education and its emerging leaders came together at what today, some seventy-five years later, is affectionately known as SOC. Back in 1949, the not-so-random confluence of New Jersey educators attending a ten-day National Camp there in the facility of Life Camps Lake Mashipacong, New York, was the beginning of something wonderful in environmental education. Dr. Vivian recalled those times in an interview for SOC: "I think we all sensed that those days were auguries of changes and growth to come—we didn't know what. We were all upwardly mobile. It was a weekend of beginnings—for SOC and many of us who were part of it."

As part of the faculty, Doc recalled the momentous occasion and his contributions,

> *All I can remember from that weekend is:*
> *1. Cleaning up and washing windows in Kittatinny Hall.*
> *2. Playing my accordion for singing—the best I could.*
> *3. Planning the summer courses.*
> *4. Building the trail to Spring Brook Cabin.*

Presently, the SOC continues to educate both the educators and the youth of today in environmental education in an outdoor environment. Dr. Vivian, impacted by another champion of EE, created a plaque that hangs on one of the walls at SOC:

> *Dr. Robert Morrison: who, as New Jersey's Assistant Commissioner for Higher Education (1945–57), believed that every pre-service teacher should have direct experiences in studying the conservation of New Jersey environments. His zeal stemmed from a conviction that the consideration of environmental learning and values is intensified in an outdoor-orientated resident program.*

Dr. Morrison was one of the invisible or not-so-invisible hands that would carry the torch or baton of environmental education and good stewardship. He was instrumental in guiding Dr. Vivian to Glassboro State College as the chairman of the Department of Science (1955–67).

This page: Young Dr. Vivian at SOC during the 1949 Memorial Day weekend celebrating the opening of SOC. *Courtesy School of Conservation.*

This page and opposite: Young Dr. Vivian at SOC during the 1949 Memorial Day weekend celebrating the opening of SOC. *Courtesy School of Conservation.*

Born in Ohio, buried at the ripe old age of eighty-nine in California, an unparalleled teacher advocate in New Jersey all his career as an educator, "Dr. Morrison was very interested in promoting environmental ed using outdoor ed as a methodology for teaching about the environment. Hands-on experiences were key ingredients in that teaching effort."

A mighty oak in his own right, Dr. Robert H. Morrison (1893–1973) had a prior working relationship with Doc in the SOC years. Dr. Morrison

ASE &
ANBORN
COFFEE

served as principal of the New Jersey State Normal School (State Teachers College) at Paterson from 1935 to 1937. Then, in 1937, he was appointed to be the state director of teacher education and subsequently, in 1945, appointed to be the assistant commissioner for higher education. It was Dr. Morrison's idea, while attending the July 1941 Education Conference at National Camp, to start a program similar to one that, at the same time, the New York Teachers College was attempting to do. The outcome was,

> *Thirty-two students assembled at National Camp for the first Camping Education Institute on June 17, 1942. The students represented a wide variety of experience, age, education, religion, and home background. Of the thirty-two from the six Teachers Colleges of the state* [Newark, Paterson, Trenton, Jersey City, Glassboro and Montclair], *eighteen had previous camp experiences either as a camper or as a counselor, and fourteen had never been to camp in any capacity.*

It wasn't just at the state level: programs like SOC were being developed as part of the environmental movement. According to this excerpt from the National Park Service website,

> *Beginning in 1967 the NPS became a leader in environmental conservation education, which then-Director George B. Hartzog, Jr. saw as crucial to the survival of the parks and the planet….Under Hartzog's direction, the NPS became a leader in the emerging Environmental Education movement in the late 1960s. In July 1967 an NPS task force released a report called* A Plan of Cooperation for Environmental Conservation. *It recommended working with schools, youth groups, public service groups, and conservation organizations throughout the country to teach children "an appreciative and critical awareness of their environment, particularly that awareness which recognizes the interactions of natural and human processes.*

An ad campaign was developed, creating Environman. Environman's message was clear in the 1970s: "You are linked to the web of life. Everything you do affects it. Everything it does affects you. Man is directly connected to his environment."

Besides an educational campaign, there was a federally funded program to identify and support environmental education centers in the private sector. The National Park Service programs National Environmental Education

Development (NEED) and National Environmental Education Landmark (NEEL) were discussed in a published paper by Frank E. Sullivan Jr. and William H. Schlesinger titled "The Environmental Education Act: Where Do We Stand Now?" (June 1972):

> *A good Environmental Education program must be conducted, in part, outside the classroom. The use of national parks, national forests and other public lands as well as city dumps, sewage treatment plants and waterways not only allows the student to see firsthand the forces interacting in his environment, but also allows him to test them and ultimately to understand them.*

Sullivan and Schlesinger offered constructive criticism and analysis to say that environmental education as a whole needed to do more. It needed to move the needle from environmental awareness and point it at an environmental understanding of man's interdependence on nature and his environment. They advocated for the expansion of the two federally funded programs. From the National Park Service website: "In 1971 a further program [NEEL] was adopted to confer national recognition on non-federal sites possessing outstanding quality for Environmental Education by designating them National Environmental Education Landmarks. Secretary of the Interior Rogers C.B. Morton designated the first eleven sites in 1971, situated in nine states and the District of Columbia."

Sullivan and Schlesinger argued that programs like those identified in the NEEL program should be expanded and held up as the right model for environmental education, with a continued focus on "curricular materials development" locally to meet the needs of the communities they were in. The NPS had already set up the NEED program, in conjunction with NEEL, to do just that. From the NPS website: "Through the National Environmental Education Development (NEED) Program, curriculum-integrating materials have been produced for A school grades kindergarten through eight. Students learn through these that nothing is static; everything is always in a state of movement and change. NEED is a multidisciplinary program."

Guess what? Dr. Vivian and the Conservation and Environmental Studies Center (CESC) staff members' environmental education program at Whitesbog Village was one of those sites chosen to be designated National Environmental Education Landmarks. Today, you can still see the bronze plaque on the outside of what today is the General Store of Whitesbog

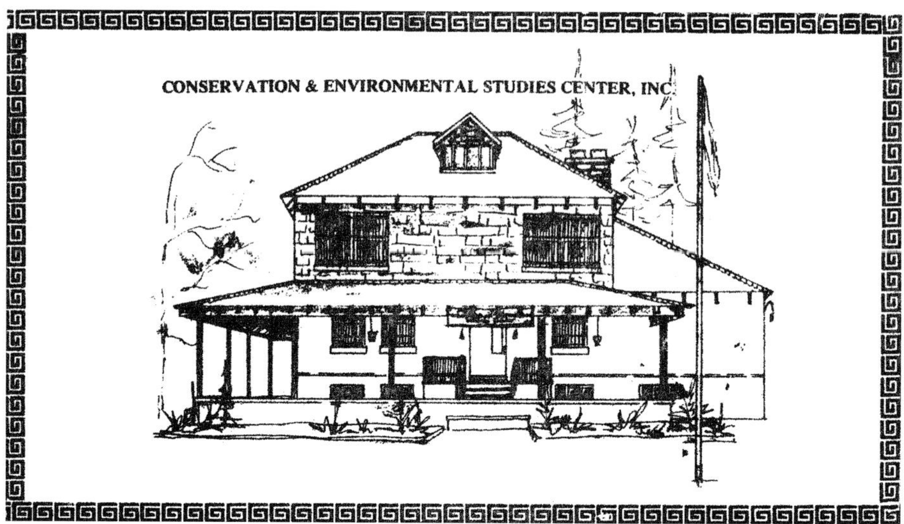

This page, top: Drawing of the Conservation and Environmental Studies Center. *From the book* Whitesbog: An Historical Sketch *(1978)*.

This page, bottom: Drawing of Norma T. Vivian Curriculum Center (artist unknown). *From the book* Whitesbog: An Historical Sketch *(1978)*.

Opposite, top: Hand-drawn map of Whitesbog Village and CESC operations circa 1978. *From the book* Whitesbog: An Historical Sketch *(1978)*.

Opposite, bottom: Topographical map of the Whitesbog Village region. *From the book* Whitesbog: An Historical Sketch *(1978)*.

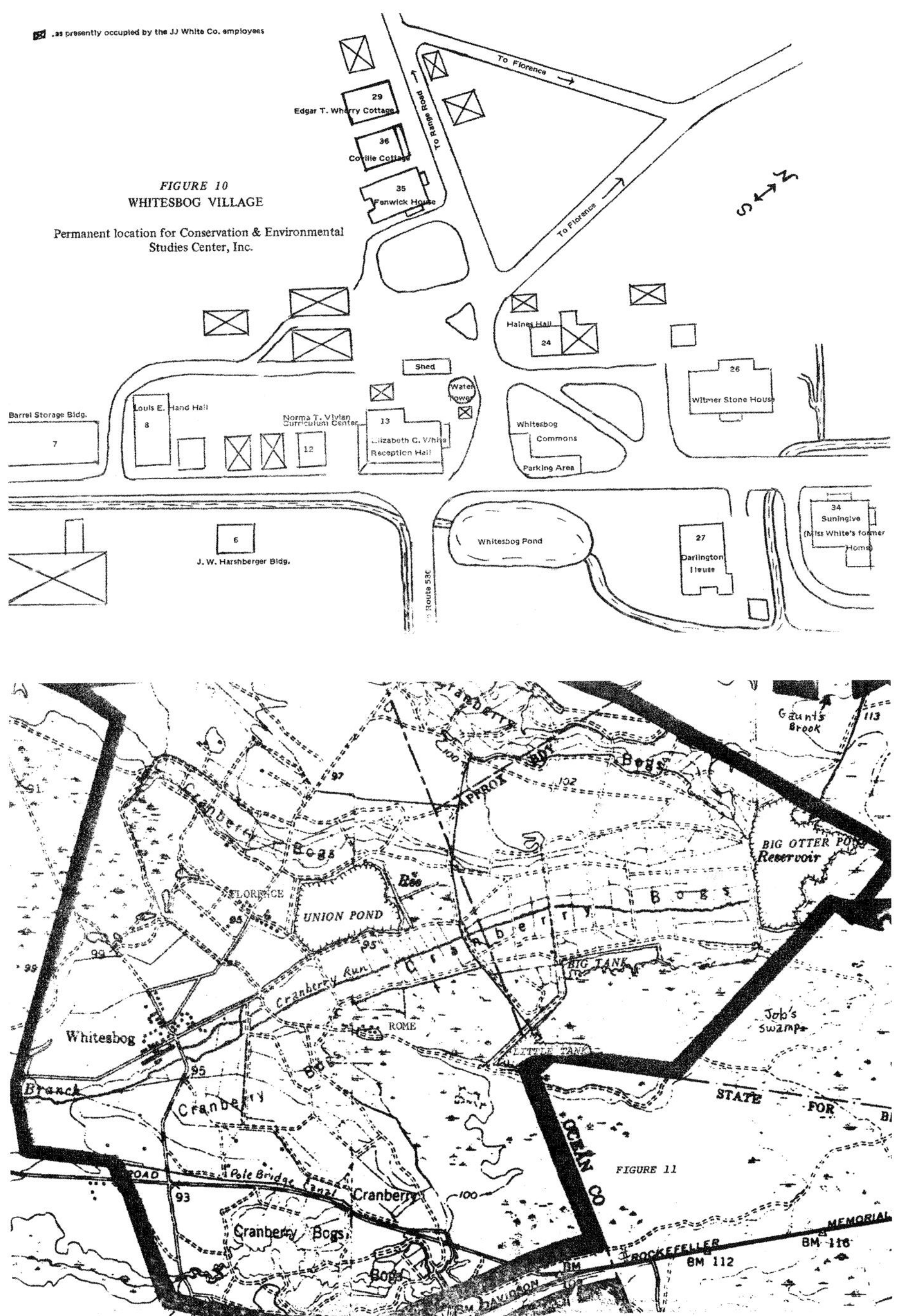

.as presently occupied by the JJ White Co. employees
FIGURE 10
WHITESBOG VILLAGE
Permanent location for Conservation & Environmental Studies Center, Inc.
To Florence
To Range Road
29
Edgar T. Wherry Cottage
36
Colville Cottage
35
Fenwick House
Haines Hall
24
Shed
Water Tower
26
Witmer Stone House
Barrel Storage Bldg.
7
Louis E. Hand Hall
8
12
Norma T. Vivian Curriculum Center
13
Elizabeth C. White Reception Hall
Whitesbog Commons
Parking Area
6
J. W. Harshberger Bldg.
Route 530
Whitesbog Pond
27
Darlington House
34
Suningive
(Miss White's former Home)
Gaunts Brook
113
97
APPROX
102
Bogs
BIG OTTER POND
Reservoir
Cranberry
Bogs
FLORENCE
UNION POND
95
Cranberry Run
BIG TANK
99
ROME
Whitesbog
LITTLE TANK
Job's Swamp
Branch
Cranberry
STATE
FOR
OCEAN CO
FIGURE 11
Pole Bridge Canal
93
Cranberry
Cranberry Bogs
100
ROCKEFELLER
MEMORIAL
BM 112
BM 116
DAVIDSON

Village, but not too long ago, it was the Conservation and Environmental Studies Center. At the time, on November 5, 1972, the *Philadelphia Inquirer* reported, "Ecology Center Wins Recognition: In making the designation, Jerry Sealoff, of the NPS, termed the center one of the finest in the country." The team at the CESC was cranking out a curriculum tailored to the Pine Barrens environment surrounding Whitesbog Village and their newly christened CESC NEEL-designated center in the Pines.

Ecology Center Wins Recognition

WHITESBOG. — The Conservation and Environmental Studies Center here, near Browns Millls, has been officially designated a National environmental Education Landmark by the National Park Service.

In making the designation, Jerry Sealoff, of the NPS, termed the center one o fthe finest in the country.

The National Park Service, in its 100th year, is in a program to recognize and encourage environmental education.

Excerpt from *Philadelphia Inquirer* on CESC's designation as a National Environmental Education Landmark (NEEL), November 5, 1972. *Author's collection.*

Sustaining winds keep the sailboat moving forward. One of the biggest gusts to fill the sails of the environmental education movement, in Doc's own words, was Earth Day 1970: "1970 was looked upon as the 'Signal Year for Environmental Education.' Although I, as well as others, had already started the recycling concept. We also advocated the fusion of outdoor education and conservation education as Environmental Education." It felt as if the tides and the winds of positive change had shifted for the environment and, more broadly, society at large, as hopes of a better future continued to fuel the passions of the teachers and environmentalists of New Jersey.

"As a college science professor in the 1960s and '70s, Vivian bridged traditional North American conservation biology with the nascent environmental movement, emphasizing field studies for students in the forests and marshes of southern New Jersey. As momentum built in the 1970s for preserving the 1 million-acre Pinelands region, several of Vivian's students became involved."* In the Pines (synonymous with "the Pine Barrens" or "the Pinelands"), environmentalists' roots found a home, gathering oxygen, fostered by a canopy of plants and the sun's rays to create sustaining energies.

* Excerpt from an August 19, 2008 *Asbury Park Press* article by Kirk Moore and Paula Scully titled "Pine Barrens Scientist, Educator Dies at 93—Bridged Conservation Biology, Environmental Movement."

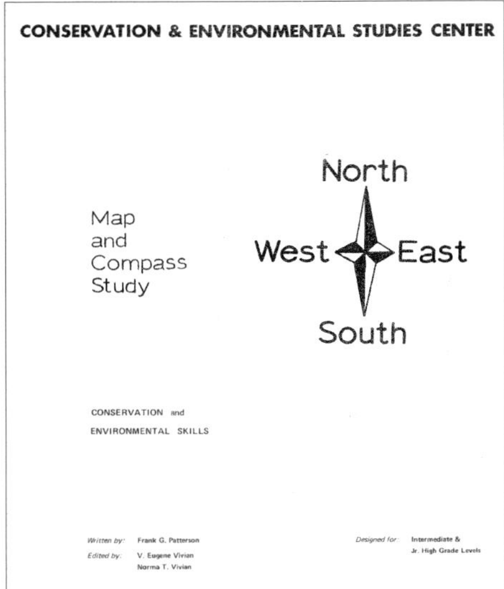

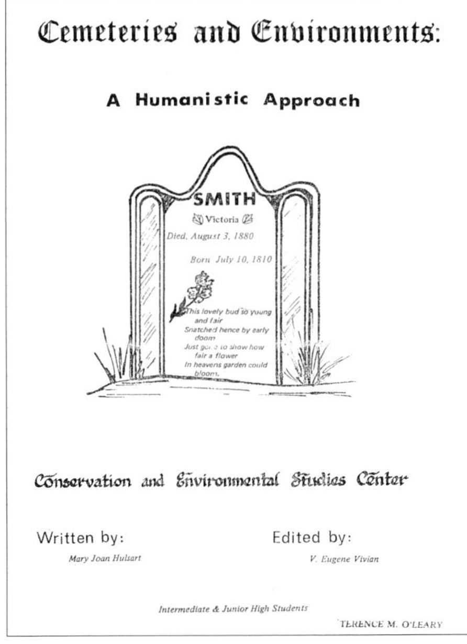

This page: Sample CESC curriculum. *Author's collection.*

A movement's creation isn't always a spark that occurs in a vacuum. On the environmental education front, many smaller events added fuel to the combustion of the movement. What follows is a short list of the major "pro-Earth" bombs that helped sustain the winds of change and fill the sails of many.

Chapter 3

ENVIRONMENTAL EDUCATION EVENTS THAT INFLUENCED OR WERE INFLUENCED BY THE LIFE OF A MIGHTY OAK, DOC VIVIAN

1899 Federal Refuse Act

1945–55 Professor Vivian teaches at Paterson State College

1948–98 Camp Pioneer is established in 1948. It ran until 1998 before being renamed and continuing mission under the name Camp Tommy in 1999. Camp Pioneer was one of the Fresh Air Fund's sleepaway camps for New York City boys ages twelve to fifteen, offering hiking and nature programs in an outdoor setting

Preserving the Pines design by Taylor Harpster. *Author's collection.*

1949 *A Sand County Almanac*, by Aldo Leopold (1887–1948), is published after his death.

1950–52 Professor V. Eugene Vivian teaches as an instructor at SOC.

1955–67 Dr. V. Eugene Vivian (he received his doctorate in 1958) serves as Science Department chairman at Glassboro State College in New Jersey.

1962 On September 27, the book *Silent Spring* by Rachel Carlson (1907–1964) is first published.

1965 President Lyndon Johnson signs the Elementary and Secondary Education Act (ESA) as part of his Great New Society program. In the legislation, outdoor education is listed as a possible fund receiver.

1966 In September, the United States Office of Education approves a planning grant of $39,000 under Title III of the Elementary and Secondary Education Act. Over the next three years, through the planning grant, subsequent allotments nearing $600,000 are awarded to the Conservation and Environmental Studies Center project. The Resident Environmental Education facility of CESC (at Methodist Conference Center at Mount Misery) served the school districts of Atlantic City, Bridgeton, Deptford, Glassboro, Salem and Willingboro.

1966 In December, Whitesbog Village (twenty-nine buildings in total) and land (2,900 acres annexed to Lebanon State Forest, which today is Brendan T. Byrne State Forest) are saved under New Jersey's Green Acres Land Acquisition Renewal Program. The buildings and land of Whitesbog Village were sold to the state of New Jersey by J.J. White Inc.

1967 John McPhee's book *The Pine Barrens* is published (parts of the book were first published in the *New Yorker*).

1967 Dr. V. Eugene Vivian steps down as Science Department chairman at Glassboro State College in New Jersey and focuses on his position as director of the Conservation and Environmental Science Center (CESC) for Southern New Jersey under a Title III–funded project (1967–71).

1967 Doc's "*Shortia galacifolia*: Its Life History and Microclimatic Requirements" is published in the *Bulletin of the Torrey Botanical Club*.

1968 On March 15, full-time operations of CESC begin, with two school classes for resident environmental education. The program took place at the facilities of the Methodist Conference Center at Mount Misery, Burlington County.

1968 On September 11, CESC is incorporated.

1969 On February 1, New Jersey Department of Conservation and Economic Development Commissioner Roe signs a twenty-five-year lease for an initial sixty-three acres at Whitesbog Village with board of trustees president Albion G. Hart and Dr. V. Eugene Vivian, executive director of CESC.

1969 From June 30 to August 8, the first summer program at Whitesbog, "Exploratory Program in Decentralized Camping for Children of Migrant Laborers," is held. The program was developed by associate director Emory J. Kiess.

1970 Vivian and Rillo write and publish curriculum titled *Focus on Environmental Education* as part of the Curriculum Development Council for Southern New Jersey.

1970 On January 1, President Nixon signs the National Environmental Policy Act.

1970 April 22 marks the first ever Earth Day and the birth of a statewide agency directed to protect the environment. Behind the wheel is Governor William T. Cahill. The New Jersey Department of Environmental Protection (NJDEP) names Richard J. Sullivan to lead the new agency.

1970 On October 7, the Federal Environmental Education Act signed into law.

1970 The Clean Air Act passes (followed by, in 1977, a congressional amendment to the Clean Air Act).

1971 The National Environmental Education Landmark (NEEL) program is created.

1971 On February 1, Doc Vivian—as executive director, after federal funds from Title III ended—founded Conservation and Environmental Studies Center Inc., a new independent nonprofit corporation providing twenty-one special environmental consultation services for public and private agencies (1971–84).

1971 Barry Commoner expands on what author Rachel Carson awakened in the public environmental consciousness in the '60s in his book *The Closing Circle: Nature, Man and Technology*.

1972 The United States bans DDT (dichlorodiphenyltrichloroethane), an insecticide used in agriculture.

1972 The National Park Service (part of the U.S. Department of the Interior) designates the Conservation and Environmental Studies Center a "National Environmental Education Landmark." The bronze plaque reads, "This site possesses distinctive values in revealing significant natural and cultural processes through effective Environmental Education programs."

1973 On March 29, the last remaining U.S. troops are removed from Vietnam.

1973 The New Jersey Endangered and Nongame Species Conservation Act is passed.

1973 *Sourcebook for Environmental Education*, authored by Dr. V. Eugene Vivian, is published.

1974 Dr. Vivian authors a book series, *Ecology for Children*, in five volumes: *Air*, *Water*, *Land*, *Plants* and *Animals*.

1978 "Congress created the Pinelands National Reserve through the passage of the National Parks and Recreation Act of 1978 and [it] is the first National Reserve in the nation. It is approximately 1.1 million acres and spans portions of seven counties and all or part of 56 municipalities" (NPS.gov).

1979 On June 28, New Jersey passes the Pinelands Protection Act (PPA), which followed President Carter's 1978 National Parks and Recreation Act.

1979 Professor Emeritus Dr. V. Eugene Vivian retires from Glassboro State College (in 1997, it becomes known as Rowan University).

1981 *Rare and Endangered Vascular Plant Species in New Jersey*, prepared by David B. Snyder and Dr. V. Eugene Vivian (Conservation and Environmental Studies Center in cooperation with the U.S. Fish and Wildlife Service), is published.

1983 Louis Dwier's book *Wilderness Wetlands in Spring: A Canoe Trip in the Pine Barrens of South Jersey* is published.

1983 Dr. Vivian becomes chairman of the Environmental Commission of Little Egg Harbor Township, Ocean County, New Jersey (1983–99).

1984 Dr. Vivian retires from CESC (1966–84).

1984 On April 1, the Cattus Island Advisory Council is established. Dr. Vivian serves on it from 1984 to 1992.

1984 Dr. Vivian founds, and leads until his retirement in 2001, ACES Environmental (Associates for Conservation and Environmental Studies).

1984 Glassboro State College continues to sponsor environmental education at Whitesbog Village, led by Professor Dr. Gary Patterson, under a new name: the Pinelands Institute for Natural and Environmental Studies (PINES).

1985 The second Annual Whitesbog Blueberry Festival is put on by Whitesbog Preservation Trust.

1988 The entire village of Whitesbog, Whitesbog Historic District, is added by the U.S. Department of the Interior to the National Register of Historic Places (NRHP).

1990 The National Environmental Education Act at the federal level moves environmental education under the purview of the EPA.

Chapter 4

BEYOND FOUR WALLS

Formative and Transitional Years of Whitesbog Village

Conservation and Environmental Studies Center, Incorporated
CESC, Inc. (1966–84)
Box 7596, RD7
Whitesbog Road
Browns Mills, New Jersey 08015

I Teach

I teach because I would be forever young in spirit and mind
Even though the passing years age my physical life
I know of no way I can remain behind and be a witness
Each passing year, but for a magic rope uncut by knife
Binds me firmly to the young minds that I love
I teach
Because I wish to fertilize the young minds I teach
With knowledge of those masters whose illuminating light
That still burns bright on the trails that wind
So torturous and steep for each young mind's mental might
Climbing ever so slowly to the uninitiated far above
I teach
Because when I pass on this flame of knowledge quest
That burns brightly with each succeeding generation
I open up their minds as if with a cognitive wedge

So that in the end they are better citizens of this nation
For this and what I have done in the service of others
I teach

—*Excerpt from the 2016 book* Not Finished Just Begun: Reflections of a Life, *by educator Dr. Thomas J. Rillo*

In all fairytales—and yes, some do come true—the story usually starts with "once upon a time," and there's always a village involved. Allow yourself to time travel back to a period in U.S. history when parts of society were in rebellion against the social norms established by previous generations affected by World War II. Most of today's generation, post–Cold War, focuses on history that they still can feel. We look for signs of the past, and usually, it's the breath of the previous generation that stirs our longing to try to keep the good and let the bad drift out to bay or sea. Sometimes we are too late to catch the essence of the previous generation, for the only traces left are their breath on the windowpanes of yesterday.

Back then, in the late 1960s, we saw and felt the emotions of a countercultural movement amped up with widespread protests against unjust wars in foreign lands, like the Southeast Asian country of Vietnam. It was a time when free-spirited and free-loving hippies were in our midst. It was there that an environmental ethos propelled by environmental educators was taking shape. Dr. Eugene Vivian and the people he surrounded himself with were of that moral fabric. The historical tapestry of New Jersey and the country was being rewoven by a new generation.

Once upon a time, there was a man like the Pied Piper of legend who masterfully brought together the most talented of teachers in a little village in the Pines. Dr. Eugene Vivian founded the New Jersey Conservation and Environmental Science Center in 1966, temporarily at Mount Misery; in 1967, he moved the CESC's staff and its important mission permanently to Whitesbog Village in Browns Mills, New Jersey. The town of Browns Mills, a vacation destination of yesterday in the 1960s, was and continues to be isolated from the rest of the state, shielded from the north by military base Joint Base McGuire-Dix-Lakehurst. An example of how great an impediment the military base has been to the area is a passive recreation Rails to Trails project that stops on the northern edge of the base and begins again in the south in the town of Pemberton, basically severing the 25.3-mile Union Transportation Trail project, even though both ends have been developed and designated for public use. In all directions, thousands

Whitesbog Village buildings by artist Lori Parsells. *Author's collection.*

upon thousands of acres of pitch pine trees and scrub oak trees known as the New Jersey Pinelands National Reserve (1.1 million acres) stretch out from the center of Whitesbog Village.

The Pine Barrens, the remotest part of the state, if known at all to the public at large, is remembered for a scene in the hit cable television show *The Sopranos* where Italian mafia members "dump the bodies" out in the Pine Barrens. Spoiler alert: that scene wasn't even filmed in New Jersey. Another Italian, with no apparent Italian accent and smaller in stature, found a home in the Pine Barrens. Doc recollected, "We used education grants from the U.S. Department of Education to set up an Environmental Education Teaching and Demonstration Center." With the teachers came the task of teaching tens of thousands of New Jersey schoolchildren in one of the most scenic and natural environments in the country.

With a plan in hand, our knight in shining armor emerged out of the darkness of despair from one of the bleakest moments for our environment, and our home, Planet Earth. Earlier in 1964, South Jersey and the New Jersey Pine Barrens faced destruction on an unheard-of level. The Pinelands Regional Planning Board was reviewing a Pinelands Jetport proposal, smack dab in the middle of our Pygmy Pine Plains in Warren Grove, New Jersey—an ecological wonder full of mysteries even today. In June 1965, the board was leaning in favor of a plan to locate in the Pines

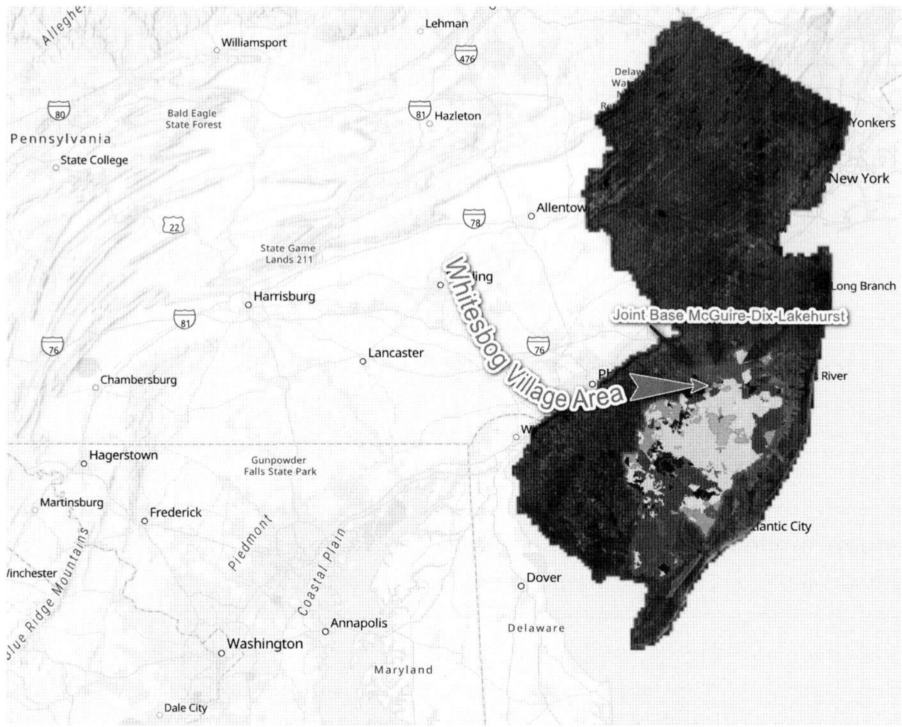

Map illustrating regional sequester from North Jersey. *Regional map rendered from State of New Jersey Pinelands Commission website, 2024.*

a "32,500-acre jetport, larger than Kennedy, LaGuardia, and Newark Airports combined, and a 10,800-acre New City along the parkway link connected with Philadelphia and New York by rail"—just twenty-two miles south of Whitesbog Village. The collation of environmental groups coming together calling for federal protection of the Pinelands became an exclamation point when author John McPhee's seminal work *The Pine Barrens* was published in 1967.

If history teaches us anything, it's that historical footnotes don't just happen overnight. Before the region became a hotbed of support for protecting the Pinelands, there was less local support for state involvement and ownership of the land. From the 2021 book *New Jersey's Lost Piney Culture*, published by The History Press: "In 1915 Wharton heirs offered the State of NJ all of 100,000 acres to the state which put it to a vote. Voters defeated the question 123,995 to 103,456 with almost all South Jersey voting against the state's purchase." Local rules and real estate values were the keys to the vote's defeat. Many locals didn't want outside intervention and enjoyed the

Wharton Estate as neighbors versus the state putting a park in there. Another question was posed to the voters:

> *In 1969, voters of Ocean and Burlington Counties answered YES or NO to the question: "Shall the Board of Chosen Freeholders of the County of ____ support the establishment of an international Jetport in the south-central area of the State of New Jersey?" The answer on November 4, 1969, was no by a margin of 2.4 no to each yes vote.*

This quote is from a 1969 Conservation and Environmental Science Center (CESC) publication authored by Frank G. Patterson, with contributions and editing by Norma T. Vivian, titled, *Exploitation of the Pine Barrens Past, Present, and Future.* Did citizens have a case of NIMBY (not in my backyard), or were they coming around to see what an environmental nightmare the jetport would be for the region? The CESC was there from the beginning, educating and changing the hearts of many about the need for preservation and improving the environment(s) of New Jersey.

The Pinelands—1.1 million acres and an evergreen sea—weren't the only threatened environment in the 1960s and '70s. Birds were dying from the use of the insecticide DDT. The skies were threatened with never having a bald eagle or osprey grace them again! Amid all this environmental degradation, and in the face of a seemingly uncaring government, came a caring human being with an academic foundation in environmental sciences and a voice and a passion for teaching. Professor V. Eugene Vivian wrote, "The deterioration of environmental quality is apparent to all citizens, yet the study of ecology and environment has not become a serious educational concern in most school districts even though there are many notable exceptions." And with mighty pen in hand, Doc developed and wrote a planning grant to fund his teaching career's greatest creation—some would say his greatest achievement, especially the tens of thousands of children who went traipsing through the village in those days and years in the enchanted forests of the Pinelands of New Jersey.

Offered up as a shimmer of hope was Title III of President Johnson's Elementary and Secondary Education Act. Through the funds received, it allowed Dr. Vivian to partner with the State of New Jersey in establishing the Conservation and Environmental Science Center (CESC), first hosted at the facilities of the Methodist Conference Center at Mount Misery, a Christian campground located in Burlington County, in 1967. After a slight name change in later years, when the mission and the CESC itself moved from Mount Misery to Whitesbog Village, it became the Conservation and Environmental Studies Center (CESC), nixing "Science" for "Studies." The CESC was opened and shuttered by a board of directors. Did the work of the CESC influence the environmental movement to preserve and protect the Pinelands from being overdeveloped and turned into a jetport, an unimaginable environmental disaster of a third metropolis on the East Coast of the United States? The CESC Center certainly did influence politicians like eco-champion Congressman James Florio (1937–2022), who visited in February 1978 to witness the programs offered by the CESC at Whitesbog Village and the teaching of Dr. Vivian and others to New Jersey schoolchildren the uniqueness of the Pinelands environment.

Many of the oak saplings or budding environmentalists in the Pine Barrens Coalition collective, based out of Vincentown, New Jersey, who were represented in the 1980–81 Pine Barrens Coalition pamphlet, echoed the sentiment felt among all who cared for the environment and the Pines: "Join the fight to save the Pine Barrens." Many of those in the coalition (fifty-six organizations) were somehow connected to the CESC and Doc, almost like the theory of six degrees of separation. At the time, Democrat Governor Brendan Byrne and Republican Congressman James Florio worked together in a nonpartisan way on legislation to save the Pine Barrens of today. The website northjersey.com has this to say about the significant event: "The Pinelands became the first national reserve in the U.S. under the National Parks and Recreation Act of 1978. It curtailed development in an effort to protect the 17-trillion-gallon Cohansey Aquifer, which provides drinking water to most of southern New Jersey. The Pinelands covers 22% of New Jersey and is home to about 700,000 year-round residents."

Chapter 5

THE VILLAGE OF WHITESBOG, BROWNS MILLS, NEW JERSEY

What Came Before

The environment that supports life extends far beyond the vision or experience of the things that live there.

—*John H. Storer*

In 1967, the village itself needed much repair from lack of use as agricultural practices changed, the buildings were no longer occupied and time took its toll on a once vibrant cranberry and blueberry farm town. The most recent guiding hand of the farming village was Elizabeth C. White (1871–1954), the eldest daughter of Joseph J. White and Mary A. Fenwick. J.J. White wrote a book on cranberry cultivation (*Cranberry Cultivation*, 1870) and was considered the New Jersey King of Cranberries even though author B. Eastwood beat him to the punch with his book *The Cranberry and Its Culture* (1856). White's eldest daughter's name is synonymous not with the cranberry but with the blueberry of today. Having helped cultivate the highbush blueberry crop with botanist and USDA agent Dr. Fredrick V. Coville, she rightly wears the crown of Blueberry Queen, ensuring both Dr. Coville and Ms. White their place in the history books.

Forgotten is that village, Whitesbog Village, and several houses of Italian migrant farming families—men, women and children—who handpicked those ruby-red cranberries for J.J. White. In 1989, then Superintendent Christian M. Bethmann of Lebanon State Forest (now Brendan T. Byrne State Forest) wrote in *The History of Lebanon State Forest*,

This page and opposite: Activities at the Conservation and Environmental Studies Center, 1979. *Courtesy O'Leary family*.

Whitesbog employed 500 pickers to harvest his cranberry crop. Most of these workers were of Italian descent, and two seasonal villages named Florence and Rome were built to house them during the harvest. The need for labor was reduced in the 1930s by the use of scoops, and again in the '50s by the development of the dry harvesting machine by Thomas Darlington, J.J.'s descendant. The development of wet harvesting techniques reduced the need for labor to the point that a half dozen men with machines can now accomplish as much as 500 hand pickers. This ended the need for the villages of Whitesbog, Florence and Rome, and in 1967 the land was sold to the State of New Jersey.

Handcrafted map predating CESC at Whitesbog Village General Store, 2024. *Author's collection.*

Forgotten, Whitesbog was destined to become a ghost town of legend. Another more famously known for documenting forgotten ghost towns of the Pine Barrens was Reverend Henry Charlton Beck. He wrote about such ghost towns in his popular book *Forgotten Towns of Southern New Jersey*. When did the thriving village of Whitesbog—some six hundred acres in total back in 1924, when J.J. White passed—become a ghost town of legend? Up until the 1950s, before the invention of the dry harvesting cranberry machine, the village and operation of J.J. White Inc. grew to almost three thousand acres. The main village, roughly sixty-three acres, had a purpose as a thriving farm town or village consisting of twenty-nine buildings. Its center was a general store that at one time also served as a post office; Suningive, the residence of the Blueberry Queen Elizabeth White, built in 1923; and on the periphery, two settlements for some two hundred Italian seasonal pickers to call home, the villages Florence and Rome, built out of white cedar, a coveted tree of the Pines.

After selling the land and buildings in December 1966 by way of New Jersey's Green Acres Land Acquisition Renewal Program, J.J. White Inc. then leased back many of the bogs and land as an active cranberry operation—then and now, in 2025. With technological improvements, what changed before the sale of the onetime home of J.J. White Inc. was the need for a village to support hundreds of migrants during the harvest season. The buildings and infrastructure to support such an enterprise weren't necessary for the future and progress of the twentieth century. This and other factors led to the decision of Tom Darlington, heir of the White family and president of J.J. White Inc., to sell to the state and lease back the land to continue the one-hundred-plus-year-old cranberry operation. By this time, all of J.J. White's family members who once lived and worked as part of the cranberry operation had moved out of Whitesbog Village down the road to Buffins Meadows. Over time and due to neglect (random acts of vandalism and arson), the no longer needed buildings and infrastructure of old Whitesbog Village started to look their age. And where there was a vacuum for want of purpose, Dr. Eugene Vivian came to provide a purpose.

Caro Suplee wrote in the *Burlington County Times* on November 6, 1988,

> *Whitesbog has endured its ups and downs. For a time, it seemed the village would crumble away, but noted environmentalist and educator Dr. Eugene Vivian established an Environmental Education center there which, for several years, gave the village new life and the schoolchildren of New Jersey a valuable lesson in a much-neglected heritage.*

Dr. Vivian received unsought public recognition in 1967, when he was named New Jersey Conservation Educator of the Year by the National Wildlife Federation, and in 1968, when he was awarded National Conservation Educator of the Year by the New Jersey State Federation of Sportsman's Clubs—this after stepping down as chairman of the Science Department at Glassboro State College, while remaining a life science faculty member, to focus on his work at the village of Whitesbog and the Conservation and Environmental Science Center (CESC). Doc had to have known he was where he was meant to be, there in the Pines of South Jersey. Conservation-minded folks serve to conserve land, while teachers like Doc know the secret to saving humanity. By way of the Earth's preservation, the only way is through awareness of our place here. A teacher opens the eyes and mind of a pupil, which leads to the heart and love.

Chapter 6

THE GREAT EXPERIMENT

What the Village Became

*"But please don't call us a nature center," asks Vivian, a bespectacled, grey-haired professor from Glassboro State College, "I'm an environmentalist, a botanist, a conservationist—but I'm not an evangelist. We are not your wild-haired, torch-brandishing environmentalists who are against everything."**

Doc knew Whitesbog Village wasn't just an old blueberry town being forgotten, adding another chapter in the popular book series of Reverend Beck appropriately titled *Forgotten Towns of Southern New Jersey*. He proposed to create an environmental studies center—not a museum, a place for outdoor environmental education—thus adding a new chapter in the village's storied past. His vision was the Conservation and Environmental Studies Center (CESC), there among the sixty-three acres of the main village, incorporating many of the old buildings with new purpose and life. Today, a visitor to Whitesbog Village in Browns Mills, New Jersey, wouldn't know where the Conservation and Environmental Studies Center (CESC) once stood, but there are clues of the past to be found by those with a historical eye. A bronze plaque, now in need of a good polish, was erected on the outside of what today is called the General Store. The building sits at the crossroads of North Whites Bogs Road and West Whites Bogs Road in Browns Mills. The

* From an article by Daisy Sharp in the *Sun Trenton Times Advertiser*, September 7, 1975.

Dr. Vivian at the Conservation and Environmental Studies Center, 1979. *Courtesy O'Leary family.*

Activities at the Conservation and Environmental Studies Center, 1979. *Courtesy O'Leary family.*

Activities at the Conservation and Environmental Studies Center, 1979. *Courtesy O'Leary family.*

plaque the only thing that exists today at the site that recognizes the vision of Dr. Eugene Vivian and the other innovative environmental educators who came through the village, passing on knowledge and educating both adults and young people alike about the impact humans have on the environment.

In his 1973 publication *Sourcebook for Environmental Education*, Doc wrote:

> *Environmental Education anywhere seeks to create a concern for all environments that leads to a commitment to preserve or develop optimum environments and improve less desirable environments. In addition, Environmental Education concerns itself with the learning environment; it seeks a commitment by educators to develop and utilize situations and conditions where learning can flourish.*

THE 1960S: FORMATIVE YEARS

Thus, Whitesbog Village was the leased vehicle by which Dr. Vivian and his team of teachers drove to a better tomorrow by planting the seeds of environmental consciousness in tens of thousands of students. Dr. Vivian

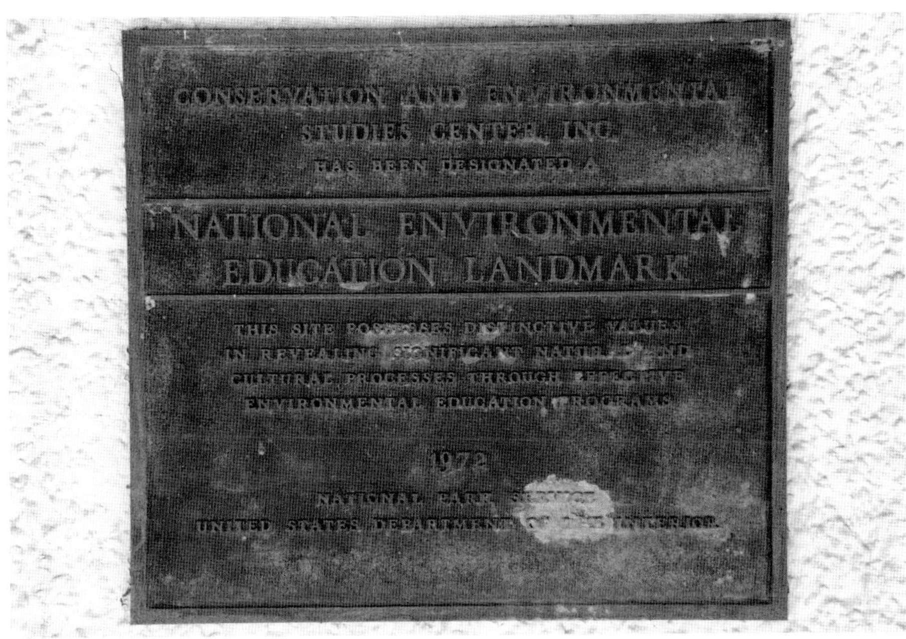

This page: National Environmental Education Landmark (NEEL), designated in 1972. *Author's collection.*

wrote in a published pamphlet dated July 1970 titled *Conservation & Environmental Science Center Whitesbog*: "In 1966, Commissioner Robert A. Roe, of the New Jersey Department of Conservation and Economic Development, and his staff endorsed leasing to CESC Inc. a portion of Whitesbog acreage as a site for a model center for environmental studies." The same pamphlet states that the site was expanded a few years later: "On February 1, 1969, Commissioner Roe and Dr. V. Eugene Vivian, founder and director of the Conservation and Environmental Science Center project, signed a 25-year lease for an initial 63 acres at Whitesbog." Just picture it: a town at a crossroads of history and possibility. One direction leads to the past; the opposite direction leads to the future; straight ahead is the federally fenced-in legendary yet forgotten pig iron–producing Pinelands town of Hanover Furnace; and behind you is the sleepy town of Browns Mills in Pemberton Township. Judith Olsen's 1976 book *Pemberton: An Historic Look at a Village on the Rancocas* paints a picture of the area so well: "The seventies brought Burlington County College, a second Pemberton Township High School, and Lake Valley Acres, and it's difficult to remember when Pemberton Manor, Pemberton Heights, and Sunbury Village were new." But she missed what was afoot at the sleepy blueberry village.

With the keys to the village, the Whitesbog Village, one man strolled down the remote sugar sand road to the future of an unconventional yet effective way to educate thousands and thousands of children and adults. The village itself consisted of "29 buildings, including processing sheds,

This page and opposite: Activities at the Conservation and Environmental Studies Center, 1979. *Courtesy O'Leary family.*

Activities at the Conservation and Environmental Studies Center, 1979. *Courtesy O'Leary family.*

barrel factory and warehouse, worker's cottages, homesteads, garages, and a former general store." The village was surrounded by hundreds of acres of cranberry bogs and roughly one hundred acres of blueberry fields, officially an annex of what was then Lebanon State Forest (now Brendan T. Byrne State Forest)—an oasis in the Pines serving as a gateway to further discovery and adventure in the southern parts of the New Jersey pine forests.

As John Cunningham put it in the 1978 book *This Is New Jersey*: "Nature, at least, knows there's a future in the Pines."

Fully funded for three years, Doc and his team of teachers got to work partnering with eighteen (eventually extending to sixty) New Jersey school districts with awarded funds to Glassboro State College under Title III of the Elementary and Secondary Education Act. The early years must have been filled with excitement for all participants. Such a remote place, in an area of sparse population: the idea didn't sell itself. Doc and his team of educators had to roll out the green pine-needle-covered carpet for the public. Curriculum writing, a strong suit of Dr. Vivian's, began immediately and never stopped. Educational material was designed to be utilized by all, from pre-K to postgraduate students and everyone in between. There was always room to improve or tailor the curriculum to an

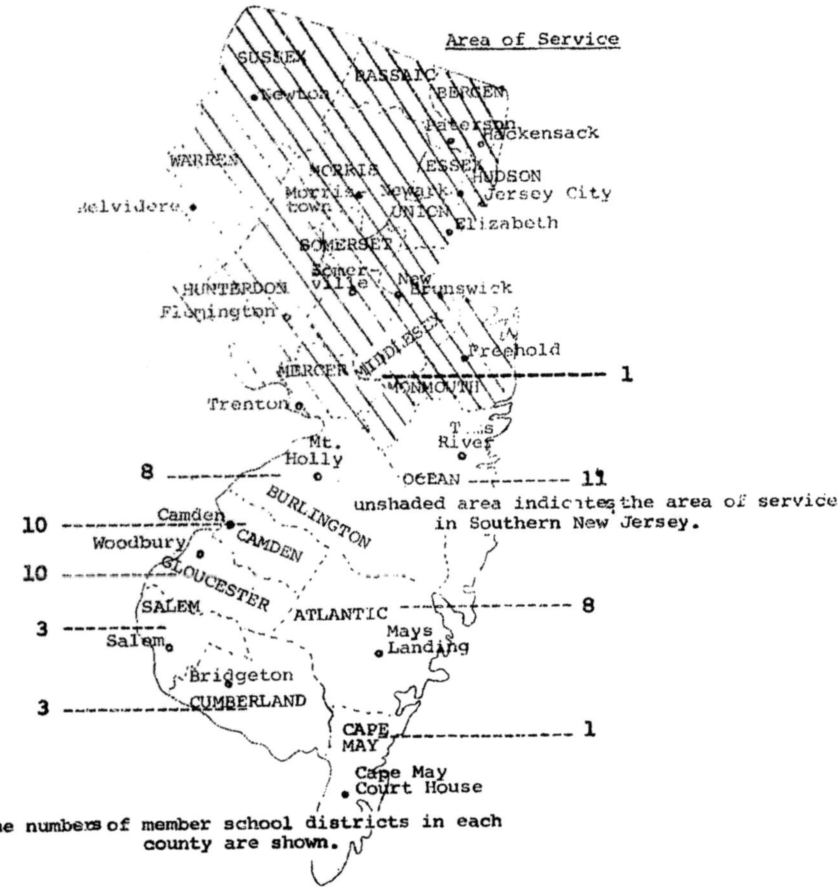

Digital map of the Area of Service rendered by the newly established Conservation and Environmental Science Center (CESC) for Southern New Jersey (1966–69). *Image credit Local Education Agency Guidebook by CESC, Inc.*

environmental need yet identified for local youth. On the very first page of every environmental education instruction plan (EEIP) school class curriculum, whether written by Doc or another CESC staff member, was a boilerplate statement from the director, Dr. Vivian. Each booklet had a quote from Doc:

> *Environmental Education has a dual nature; it strives:*
> *to create a concern for all environments that leads to a commitment to preserve optimum environments and improve less desirable environments.*
> *to utilize the most favorable learning environment possible.*

PLEASE READ BEFORE PROCEEDING

Dear Environmental Educator:

This Environmental Education Instruction Plan (EEIP) has been prepared in answer to the demand for usable curriculum materials for developing environmental awareness in today's students.

Environmental education has a dual nature; it strives:

to create a concern for all environments that leads to a commitment to preserve optimum environments and improve less desirable environments.

to utilize the most favorable learning environment possible.

To implement this commitment, this EEIP was designed as a series of indoor-outdoor-indoor experiences, which are utilized to develop one or more concerns for the quality of the environment. Each lesson was designed to build on the learnings of the previous lessons, to foster the measurement and achievement of the behaviorally stated goals of instruction.

In order that these step-by-step learnings occur, it is strongly recommended that this EEIP be adopted (or adapted) in its entirety, rather than being used solely as a source for a few outdoor activities.

Since the Conservation and Environmental Studies Center is vitally interested in suggestions for further improvement of our curriculum offerings, may we ask that you, our reader, please complete and send to us the evaluation form enclosed with this EEIP.

Cordially,

V. Eugene Vivian

V. Eugene Vivian, Ph.D.
Director

Environmental Education Instruction Plan (EEIP) sample. *Author's collection.*

This set the stage for EE learning at Whitesbog Village and the CESC. And each teacher's EEIP school class curriculum was attached to an evaluation form requesting suggestions for ways to improve the EE offerings for the community it served. Under Dr. Vivian's leadership, fifteen detailed curriculum guides were written. Dr. Vivian is quoted here by Rae Walton in *The Ancestry of Vincent Eugene Vivian*:

> *We distributed a catalog of "day lessons" which described the learnings, which were to take place in the Center. It was not just a "Show and Tell" program but a program where the children were introduced to different types*

> *of learning activities where they would observe, measure, and do something about some aspect of the environment. The catalogue contained some seventy activities from which children and teachers could make a selection. The Center Staff also wrote fifteen detailed curriculum guides for topics such as "Water Quality Monitoring." One of the last curriculum productions of the Center was to produce a recycling education program for schools of the State of New Jersey named "Here Today, Here Tomorrow" to verbalize the notion that trash material never goes away and hopefully can be used more than one time or re-manufactured into something to be used again.*

This linked the CESC and Glassboro State College to the districts stretching across the state, not just in the Pinelands region. And while Doc's dream of an out-of-door village to educate the masses in environmental education was moving full steam ahead, he was also administrating and directing the Experienced Teacher Fellowship Program at SOC. That was a direct result of his cowriting a proposal that received a grant from Title V of the Higher Education Act. With the support of his second wife, Norma T. Vivian, he could accomplish anything he set his mind to: "Always looking for an opportunity to aid me in my Environmental Education efforts, she successfully induced the *Gloucester County Times* of Woodbury to sponsor me as their nominee for New Jersey's Conservation Educator of the Year, 1967. Her success was evidenced by my being named both State and National Conservation Educator of the Year (State, 1967; National, 1968)."

Norma T. Vivian. *Courtesy George and Nadine Young.*

During this time, things were going great for the couple, both professionally and in their personal lives. With the numerous awards and the help of his wife and family, Doc was able to continue the mission of the CESC even as the federal dollars ran out. Norma expertly edited all the curriculum generated by the CESC, and some of the material still exists in practice today. She was a fan of Appaloosa horses, and it may have been on the back of one of those beautifully spotted horses, while taking a horseback riding skill course at Whitesbog, that she died suddenly from heart issues on March 11, 1972. Dr. Vivian, a dedicated family man, was deeply affected by this severe tragedy.

THE 1970s: GOLDEN YEARS OF CESC TEACHING EXPERIENCE

It's sweet to the feet: that's why they call it sugar sand. The sun had just come up over the active cranberry bog as George Young, stepson of Dr. Vivian, walked out the front door of the Darlington House, located in the southeast of the village (he also lived on the northwest side of town, in the Coville Cottage, at one time). The young man started to make his way down the dirt road, heading in a westerly direction, with his two German shepherd dogs. He was joined momentarily by another smiling staff member, standing in his hiking boots just across the street: neighbor and fellow CESC teacher Terry O'Leary. O'Leary was renting the four-bedroom Witmer Stone House from the CESC. Terry's dog, Eskimo Spitz, greeted the other two dogs excitedly while the two men exchanged good mornings and began the march down the sand road, passing a single row of metal mailboxes before coming to the end of the road. There in the Whitesbog Commons area, the two would find their other coworker, local elementary school science teacher George Henkel, who was in his thirties too. George's cedar shake–adorned home with a red tin roof also had the secondary purpose of being the CESC's library, aptly named the Fenwick House. The three sets of boots—and too many paws to count—didn't dally long, making quick work of the sugar sand walking down the road to what was once the General Store, now the Elizabeth C. White Reception Hall, to get ready to greet a new busload of children and local schoolteachers from around the region. All three of these teachers went on to get their master's degrees together at Glassboro State College.

George Young remembers,

> *We were all great friends. Several of us went to college together. George Henkel, Terry O'Leary, and I went and got our master's degree together. I used the GI Bill and got $200 a month or something. I was living and working at Whitesbog and drove out to Glassboro State College (since 1997, Rowan University) 3, sometimes 4, times a week at night. I first started at Burlington County Community College but transferred over.*

Dr. Vivian, who housed himself in Elizabeth White's old home, Suningive, would already have checked the day's schedule of groups coming to visit. One of the three teachers would go into the adjacent cedar shake operations building with the wooden name placard "Norma T. Vivian Curriculum

Circa 1990s photo of Witmer Stone House. *Courtesy O'Leary family.*

Center" hanging on the wall outside (so named after Dr. Vivian's second wife, Norma Vivian, who had died in Whitesbog Village from a horse-riding-related accident) and get materials for the day. It was just another typical start to a day in the Pines educating the masses while keeping an eye on the grasses for wood ticks!

That was the routine for several years for the teachers who looked to Doc as a mighty oak and beloved mentor—not to mention the boss of CESC Inc. Dr. Vivian was the boss, but during his entire tenure guiding the center's activities, he did not take a salary, for he was already being paid by Glassboro State College. And for the other teaching staff of the center employed by CESC, it was more economical to rent the cedar-shake homes that made up the village than to commute from somewhere else. The teacher's salary and the remoteness of the village lent themselves to the need to stay on-site, which also helped extend the life of homesteads that needed updating and continuous care. Out of necessity, the renters were required to do any needed maintenance to the homes they lived in at their own cost. Many residents of the village shared the same ubiquitous stories of the hardships Father Time and rampant vandalism had visited on various unoccupied buildings. At the time, there were many buildings outside Whitesbog Village in the old Italian migrant farmworker towns of Florence and Rome—two-story homes painted into the landscape, now lingering on only in the history of the past.

This page: CESC staff party, June 1974, at Suningive in Whitesbog. *Courtesy O'Leary family.*

What an experience it must have been for a nature enthusiast and teacher of environmental education to live in the environment they loved and taught others, children and adults, to love, too! The honeymoon period ended as the federal funds drew to an end in the early 1970s, which is when Doc began to diversify CESC's offerings even more so that the center could continue to thrive, not just survive. For her 1978 book *Whitesbog: An Historical Sketch*, Barbara V. Michalsky interviewed Dr. Vivian and questioned the expansion of duties and programs to support the CESC. Dr. Vivian spelled out the program's main purpose:

> *It is the central purpose of CESC to supply a research and development function in education. Sporadic R and D inputs come from college and universities, but the education industry—school boards and school systems—has not usually been willing or able to support what every other industry has recognized as its lifeline—research and development.*

Dr. Vivian would agree with the sentiment expressed by author Frederick Elder when he said, "It is the very segmentation of life without the desire or effort to see or appreciate its unity which is a central point of contention for those who see life as a web and not like separate folders in a file drawer." Dr. Vivian had no qualms about recruiting experts in various scientific fields to supplement what he and his team at the CESC knew. And as he expanded operations to include consulting, his network or life web enabled him to accomplish so much more than the proverbial mighty oak standing alone in the middle of a field.

At the heart of any institution is the art of preserving what is for future generations to cherish and learn from. Whitesbog Village before the CESC was the birthplace of the modern-day blueberry. Doc felt he had a duty and responsibility to save what there was and to continue to build on the place's history. Evidence of this was reported in the 2013 *Whitesbog Preservation Trust Newsletter*. Speaking of the account that took place in the 1970s is botanist and local teacher Ted Gordon:

> *The late Dr. Eugene Vivian, Director of the Conservation and Environmental Studies Center (CESC) then housed at Whitesbog, and I had just concluded a botanical walk along the cranberry bog dikes. We returned to the Elizabeth C. White Reception Hall (the old General Store) to greet June* [Vail] *at the appointed time. She had come to CESC with a donation of two cranberry crates laden with historic Whitesbog photographs, documents, ledgers, letters, magazine and newspaper articles, and memorabilia. During an hour's conservation with June, I learned that she had already made similar and even more significant and extensive donations a number of years earlier.*

This story shared by Ted Gordon of his brief encounter with June Vail is one of many examples of executive director Dr. V. Eugene Vivian serving as curator, preservationist and protector of the history of not just Whitesbog Village but also the Pinelands. Doc's time spent at Whitesbog Village demonstrated that sometimes people are caught up in something bigger than themselves and, thankfully, the right people are in the right place at the right time. Where would all those historical documents about the beginnings of cultivated blueberry history, the life of Elizabeth Coleman White and the Whitesbog Historical Archives at Whitesbog Village be if the CESC didn't exist at the time and June Vail had not had the fortitude and smarts to save the history of a place she loved dearly? June Mershon Vail (1922–2012) was a close aide and friend to Elizabeth White for nine years but also a person of historical significance, helping the history of yesteryear continue to inspire future generations as a firsthand witness and keeper of the light of history.

Without those crates of "Whitesbog historic photos, documents, ledgers, letters, magazine and newspaper articles and memorabilia" from that 1970s encounter Ted Gordon described and other acts over Doc's seventeen-year tenure, Whitesbog Village's history wouldn't be as bright. Only a person of vision like Dr. Vivian could see the value of preserving and passing on the history of the place in addition to the importance of protecting the natural habitat surrounding the village. The CESC staff and Dr. Vivian should be thanked for their historical preservation efforts and lasting contributions, then and now, toward ensuring that records of Elizabeth White's life and the daily lives of those who spent time in the cranberry company town are preserved. Archives can be saved, and they can be thrown away. Thankfully, Dr. Vivian and his team were in the mindset of saving history as much as they were in the business of saving the environment.

On a walk down Whites Bogs Road, a sugar sand road in Browns Mills, New Jersey, let your mind wander and wonder, taking you back in time to simpler days and ways, for this road is full of historical significance. If walls could talk, the village buildings of old Whites Bog Village could tell a story of those who lived in a different time. History and those who record it search for notable periods that have a beginning and an end. Where one stage or, in this case, one evergreen wave forms, crests and dissipates, there is a lifetime of memories and accomplishments. It is the beginnings and the ends of history that perpetuate our present into the future. Without knowing, we start from scratch. Preservation and pride in what came before were part of the ethos of what Dr. Vivian and the team at CESC had created there in the Pines. Dr. Vivian, in his 2003 autobiography *The Ancestry of Vincent Eugene Vivian*, said,

> *For the Center at Whitesbog we used Title III money to renovate the General Store and a couple of other buildings to produce facilities for classes with an auditorium-like room in part of the storage area of the general store. Other buildings restored and renovated included the old "boarding house" as they called it, which we fixed up to use to entertain visitors who came to Whitesbog to observe the famous Whitesbog Method of cranberry culture. Another was the "barrel factory" used as an auxiliary classroom. Whitesbog was so named because it was the farm-plantation of Joseph J. White and Sons. Elizabeth White, the daughter of Joseph, conceived the idea of developing the blueberry for commerce, which she did in concert with Dr. Frederick Coville, of the USDA. They hybridized several blueberry plants to produce the super-sized berries known today. That story was always part of our presentation to the classes.*

From the beginning, Doc's goal was to preserve and to build on what existed in the village at the time. He was the team captain and the only staff member. "The CESC: A Progress Report" (1969) documented the following:

> *Planning conferences for Environmental Education, teacher in-service and administrative workshops were conducted during the period from September 1966 to December 1967. Dr. Vivian, the project's sole staff member during planning, was released from most administrative and teaching responsibilities by the college in order to direct the development of the Conservation and Environmental Science Center for Southern New Jersey (CESC).*

On March 15, 1968, full-time operation of the CESC commenced. Documented in the aforementioned progress report are the names of the supporting original team: associate director Emory J. Kiess and staff teachers Fred J. Mason, Frank G. Patterson, John D. Raffo, Lois M. Schoeck, John E. Hiros, Karen M. Ambry and John Y. Jackson. Over the years, CESC stretched too few dollars to support a roster of innovative and dedicated environmental educators not listed previously, including but not limited to Dr. Ambry, Dr. Rillo, Terry O'Leary, George Henkel, Joe Palumbo, Howard Boyd, Donna McBride, David Snyder, Lenny Little and George Young. The list goes on and on. Doc himself did not take a salary; he lived off the salary from Glassboro State College at the time. The Conservation and Environmental Science Center's Whitesbog 1970 pamphlet mentions a far grander scale of the enterprise that was envisioned but never materialized. If Doc's dream was fully realized, it would have looked like this:

> *Permanent buildings for CESC will be erected in the vicinity of an existing air strip and reservoir. The complex will provide a dining hall, library, dormitories, infirmary and office building, as well as research laboratories. The projected buildings have been designed by the architect-conservationist, Malcolm B. Wells, of Cherry Hill. His dynamic designs demonstrate an ecological harmony with the landscape at Whitesbog. The unique construction is projected to meet the needs of the 21st century, and suggest a revolutionary concept for future architecture.*

What a site this would have been if only sufficient funding were attained!

Several festive events took place during Doc's tenure at Whitesbog Village. One was a wedding—but technically not the first, since Doc had gotten married in the village earlier on in 1972 (more on that to come). The second event was a recurring event, a favorite pastime of Doc and many others: square dance gatherings. George Young, Doc's stepson, got married at Elizabeth White's home in Suningive in 1976. Guests dressed in their finest attire walked the sugar sand road down to the company town store just past the Whitesbog Commons intersection in the village, where the wedding reception was hosted in today's General Store.

George Young had been living with his parents in the Suningive homestead before marriage, and after, he and his wife, Nadine, moved to the Coville Cottage, right next to the old schoolhouse. George recollects,

> *Dr. Vivian and the staff named all the buildings after famous botanists or ecologists. A lot of the houses needed quite a bit of work to be habitable. We fixed the walls, painted the house, fixed the heater, windows, etc. Lived there for 2 or 3 years. We'd be sitting in the living room at night and watching TV, and a bat would fly by our head. We'd catch it and let it go. The next day, more bats were flying in. They went up in the attic of the house, which mostly had sawdust for insulation. We discovered thousands of bats in the attic. Someone from the state came up, closed the entire house off and sprayed the attic with cyanide to kill all the bats. We were out of the house for a couple of weeks and stayed at Suningive for a while. The attic caught fire later in the 1970s.*

Above: Marie Vivian; her son George Young; his bride, Nadine Young, and Dr. Vivian at Suningive, November 23, 1975. *Courtesy Nadine & George Young.*

Right: Bride and groom Nadine and George Young at Suningive, November 23, 1975. *Courtesy Nadine & George Young.*

Left: Bride and groom Nadine and George Young at Suningive, November 23, 1975. *Courtesy Nadine & George Young.*

Right: Newlyweds Nadine and George Young dancing at the Elizabeth C. White reception hall, November 23, 1975. *Courtesy Nadine & George Young.*

George and his beloved Nadine are still married today—going on forty-eight years as of 2024. They physically retired to Tennessee, but their hearts are still in Browns Mills, New Jersey, and the Pinelands National Reserve. Doc himself had gotten married at Suningive to George's mother, Marie Young (née Perira), in 1972. Pemberton Township mayor, Glassboro College colleague and friend Frederick M. Detrick Jr. ticked off one more duty as he presided over the marriage between Dr. Vivian and his third wife, Marie A. Young, at Whitesbog Village. As Doc tells it:

> *Marie and I met by happenstance at the home of Nickki Press, her sister, and a friend of Norma's who operated a sewing center in Tuckerton. In three months, Marie was urging that we marry. A psychologist-trained friend from the Glassboro faculty, whose opinion was that we not waste time to establish a respectful interval following Norma's passing, encouraged us. We were married on the 8th of October, 1972, on a warm sparkling day in the east field (yard) of "Suningive," the Vivian family home. We honeymooned in Barbados.*

If you've ever visited an active cranberry farm in rural South Jersey, you'll understand how quickly feelings can develop and last for a lifetime between you and a place you just met. A love affair is easily kindled in places such as Whitesbog Village in the Pines. That remoteness provided an idyllic setting, yet it isn't for everyone, as Daisy Sharp of the *Sun Trenton Times Advertiser* reported on September 7, 1975:

> *"It's rural living," said Tom Griffin, the* [CESC] *center's curriculum and instruction administrator, public relations man, and general jack of all trades. "Supermarkets are half an hour away and the closest towns were two derelict migrant camps, Florence and Rome, named by Italian farmworkers. The state burned down Rome and knocked down Florence. They simply didn't have the money to keep up the houses."*

But for many, the country bumpkin pineball-loving (pineball = pinecone) lifestyle—the Piney life—is worth an extra thirty-minute ride to get to civilization. It's the perfect backdrop for the festive events mentioned earlier, weddings and square dance gatherings. V. Eugene Vivian, Doc, loved square dances, and they served as a way to expand public offerings at the village in

Rome village building fire of 1969. *Courtesy the O'Leary family.*

Rome village building fire of 1969. *Courtesy O'Leary family.*

Browns Mills. Doc's daughter-in-law Nadine Young, in a 2024 interview, spoke about those days fondly,

> *Anybody that would want to come, that wanted to listen to the music at night, was invited to our events. When I lived there, most of the people worked at the CESC. We knew everybody, and everyone got along, a very happy family. We all worked together, and we played together. Events were always going on. I remember we hosted various Piney bands.*
>
> *But there's no experience better than living in Whitesbog. I'm not as experienced as the others in plants and such. Not only the plants but just walking through the bogs. The blueberry fields and the cranberry fields. You could walk for miles and miles. We had dogs, and my family would come out and we'd take long walks in the bogs. Florence was there, and Rome was still there, too. It was very sad when Florence was taken down by the state out on the airfields. I was never a history buff. But the size of it—there's nothing better. Then having all that area as your backyard that just went on forever. And with George, I'd bring my family, and he'd point out the flowers, the plants and the trees. You couldn't beat the experience. I don't think you could get a better spot. It wasn't just Whitesbog; it was the pygmy pine forest and so many other places in the Pinelands that you could go to,*

Sam Hunt playing the banjo in the Pineconers band at a CESC event in Whitesbog Village, June 1978. *Courtesy O'Leary family.*

Young and old gather to listen to some old-timey Piney music by the Pineconers at a CESC event in Whitesbog Village, June 1978. *Courtesy O'Leary family.*

Top: Young and old gather to listen to some old-timey Piney music by the Pineconers at a CESC event in Whitesbog Village, June 1978. *Courtesy O'Leary family.*

Bottom: Pineconers band playing at CESC, June 1978. *Left to right*: David Rinear, Janice Sherwood, Gladys Eayre, Sammy Hunt. *Courtesy O'Leary family.*

Top: Gladys and Sammy playing at a CESC event in Whitesbog Village, June 1978. *Courtesy O'Leary family*.

Bottom: David Rinear playing the mandolin in the Pineconers band at a CESC event in Whitesbog Village, June 1978. *Courtesy O'Leary family*.

Shades of Yesteryear -
Proud To Be A Piney

Proud to be a Piney
(Lilli Lopez version)
1. There's a place that I know
where the tall pinetrees grow
and the breezes blow off of the bay.
It's the one place for me --
it is where I want to be
and I hurry back whene'er I go away.
CHORUS:
Guess I was a Piney from the start
and proud to be a South Jersey Piney in the heart
of that place that I know
where the tall pinetrees grow
and breezes blow off of the bay.
2. There's an old house in town
that has since tumbled down,
where little children played around the yard.
With a Mother and Dad,
the best we could have had;
they gave us all they could tho' times were hard.
REPEAT CHORUS
3. At our Dad's hand we learned
self respect has to be earned.
"Be proud of who you are," he'd often say.
For when you leave this ol' earth
the name you've made is all you're worth.
It was his legacy when he was called away.
REPEAT CHORUS
4. Since the bulldozers came
the town is not the same.
New houses far as I can see.
They're mushroomed 'long the shore,
I don't know it anymore;
still it's my home and where I'll always be.
REPEAT CHORUS
- Lillian Arnold Lopez "Pineylore"

"Proud to Be a Piney" song lyrics from the book Pineylore by Lillian Arnold Lopez. *Author's collection.*

> *like Pasadena. You could go on and on. George Henkel and Terry O'Leary and the other folks that worked at CESC made it such an exciting time, too.**

One of those bands was the bluegrass band called the Pineconers. In the Pines today, they're considered one of the originals. One must remember that back then, local bands in the Pines were adapting their music to the times. The proposed jetport to be built in the Pine Barrens, creating a third city in the triangle of confluence on the East Coast, had many but not all locals riled up. The powers that be wanted to pave over the pygmy pines of Warren Grove and create a city to rival Philadelphia and New York City. The publication of John McPhee's 1967 book *The Pine Barrens*, among other significant events, caused an avalanche or evergreen tidal wave of public pushback. The music of the Pines, or what was fostered out of the Albert Brothers' hunting cabin, came once a week: the Saturday night show titled *Sounds of the Jersey Pines*. Along with the banjo twang and sultry voices of Gladys Eayre and Janice Sherwood, the Pineconers band and other local musicians' music had a pro-environmental message. They and many others didn't want "paradise in the pines" paved over. Dr. Vivian and the CESC would host them and many other Piney bands at night programs in the village or on weekends at either Whitesbog or at the Christian camp Pinelands Center at Mount Misery, established in 1947 just down the road, which regularly hosted students for three days and two-night environmental education classes like the CESC's.

* Nadine Young, age seventy-three, personal communication, January 8, 2024.

Chapter 7

THEN AND NOW, BEACONS OF HOPE

The Village Buildings

The memories of those who lived it were surveyed to see who said it first. It was well known and repeatedly said by the folks who knew Doc best that he was a mighty oak that had many acorns fall from his limbs. The honor of saying it first has to go to Dr. Robert Elder, who was quoted in Bob Birdsall's 2007 book *People of the Pines*, in the section on environmental educator and mentor V. Eugene Vivian, PhD: "Eugene Vivian planted many acorns that grew into mighty oaks."

He did so as a Boy Scout Acorn Leaf awardee around 1915 and one who went on to get his master's in botany in 1940, subsequently writing his doctorate thesis about plants and soil, *Scientific Principles Underlying the Conservation of Soils, Forests, and Grasslands*, in 1958 and doing postdoctorate work in chemistry in 1960 at the University of Montana in Bozeman. With his accumulated knowledge of and interest in plants (in 1981, he coauthored the book *Rare and Endangered Vascular Plant Species in New Jersey* with the U.S. Fish and Wildlife Service), is it a surprise that Doc would name the buildings that comprised the operation he founded and ran for nearly twenty years at Whitesbog Village after people of the environmental education movement?

This page: Curlygrass fern, *Schizaea pusilla*. *Author's collection.*

This page: Curlygrass fern, *Schizaea pusilla*. *Author's collection.*

The village of today: Edgar T. Wherry Cottage. *Credit Dennis McDonald.*

The Edgar T. Wherry Cottage

The Edgar T. Wherry Cottage is the last one on the left before you hit Range Road heading northeast from the village. George Young remembers, back in his time spent living and working at the CESC, the discovery of greenhouses behind the Wherry Cottage. It was named for a guy who "dug" ferns more than anyone else and enjoyed a good pitcher plant. According to Wikipedia, "Edgar T. Wherry (1885–1982) was an American mineralogist, soil scientist and botanist. He had a deep interest in ferns and sarracenia."

The Coville Cottage

"Coville" is a no-brainer when looking for heroes and heroines to represent the outdoor movement. At home, in the field of blueberry cultivation, Frederick Coville spent many a day at Whitesbog Village with Elizabeth White propagating and hybridizing wild huckleberry bushes into the highbush blueberry industry standards of today. Most in New Jersey know only of his work with the little blue sapphires, but his life's accomplishments dwarf that footnote in his history. From Wikipedia:

The village of today: Coville Cottage. *Credit Dennis McDonald.*

Frederick Vernon Coville (March 23, 1867–January 9, 1937) was an American botanist who participated in the Death Valley Expedition (1890–1891), was honorary curator of the United States National Herbarium (1893–1937), worked at then was chief botanist of the United States Department of Agriculture (USDA), and was the first director of the United States National Arboretum. He contributed to economic botany and helped shape American scientific policy of the time on plant and exploration research.

The village of today: Fenwick House. *Credit Dennis McDonald.*

The Fenwick House

The name Fenwick House is another attempt to pay homage to those residents of Whitesbog Village who came before. Mary A. Fenwick and Joseph Josiah White were the parents of future Blueberry Queen Elizabeth C. White. But the name also lends a nod to founding family member Colonel James Fenwick. As reported by Sally Friedman of the *New York Times* in 1993: "Whitesbog was founded in 1857 by Col. James Fenwick as a 100-acre experimental cranberry farm and continued by his daughter and son-in-law, Mary Fenwick and Joseph Josiah White."

The Haines Hall

The Haines Hall was named after Isaiah Haines, vice president and general manager of the White Company, who worked there for a total of fifty-eight years. It was renovated and put into use in September 1970 honoring "Mr. Isaiah Haines…who serves as a resource person for school and adult groups visiting CESC's temporary resident Environmental Education

The village of today: Haines Hall. *Credit Dennis McDonald.*

program center at Mount Misery, or the day field study programs conducted at Whitesbog."

The Witmer Stone House

Witmer Stone House is named after Witmer Stone. According to Wikipedia, "Witmer Stone (September 22, 1866–May 24, 1939) was an American ornithologist, botanist, and mammalogist. He worked for over 51 years in the Ornithology Department at the Academy of Natural Sciences of Philadelphia and served in multiple roles, including director from 1925 to 1928."

The Darlington House

Darlington House is quite possibly named after Thomas Darlington, who was J.J. White's great-grandson and inventor of the mechanical cranberry scoop,

Above: The village of today: Witmer Stone House. *Credit Dennis McDonald.*

Left: The village of today: Darlington House. *Credit Dennis McDonald.*

which caused a dramatic change in the landscape during the fall harvest season. Imagine one device replacing hundreds of hand pickers, along with the wooden scoop cranberry workers. There was no longer a need for a great deal of migrant worker housing, as the workforce was reduced to a handful of farmhands. The Darlington House, the Witmer Stone House and Elizabeth White's home, Suningive, were considered administrators' homes by the CESC team under Dr. Vivian.

Suningive

Suningive, the former home of Elizabeth White, was built in 1923. According to Wikipedia, "Elizabeth Coleman White (October 5, 1871–November 11, 1954) was a New Jersey agricultural specialist who collaborated with Frederick Vernon Coville to develop and commercialize a cultivated blueberry."

George Young, who lived for a period in his early twenties at the house, called it the Suningive or Upside-Down House. "It's called that because the kitchen was on the second floor rather than on the first floor," he said. "When it was used as a cranberry and blueberry plantation, they used the first floor for an infirmary for Whitesbog. They had an elevator to the second and third floor, which was Elizabeth White's bedroom. Most of the living quarters were on the second floor, like the bedrooms and kitchen."

The Water Tower

The water tower supplied all the water for the main section of Whitesbog and the Italian migrant farmworker residences of Florence and Rome. It held approximately thirty thousand gallons of water. John Joyce, resident of Whitesbog Village for nine years and Buildings Committee chair for thirty years, until 2023, recalls a story connected to the water tower.

> *There was a hole in the roof with a drop ceiling underneath over the actual tank under the roof. The birds were all nesting on the drop ceiling and defecating in the water. At one point, I was offered a month's rent free if I went up and dropped two gallons of bleach in the water tank. I was barely making minimum wage with the army* [as a civilian employee]. *This*

This page: The village of today: Suningive, home of Elizabeth C. White. *Credit Dennis McDonald.*

Circa 1990s photo of water tower at Whitesbog Village, which supplied drinking water to residents. *Courtesy O'Leary family.*

is a weird story. The night before I was going to do that, I got a call from an old girlfriend from Illinois. She asked me if I was doing OK. I said I was alright, and she said, "I had a dream last night that you climbed up this big, tall tower and you fell off. I told her, "That's funny, I'm going up a tall tower tomorrow—but I'll be really careful, I promise." I tell this to my girlfriend at the time, who's now my wife of forty years. I tell her the story, and she freaks out and tells me not to go up that tower. But I said, "Are you kidding? I'm getting a month's rent off for this." So I went up, dumped the two gallons of bleach and came back down. The state replaced that tank. The structural tower is still the original, but in 1991, they replaced the tank. But yeah, it was a horror story: the water got horribly polluted. I never drank that water, but I washed with it.

The Elizabeth C. White Reception Hall

The first permanent building at the new CESC, the Elizabeth C. White Reception Hall, was named in honor of Elizabeth White. From Wikipedia: "Elizabeth Coleman White (October 5, 1871–November 11, 1954) was a New Jersey agricultural specialist who collaborated with Frederick Vernon Coville to develop and commercialize a cultivated blueberry."

Today, it serves as a multiuse building for the Whitesbog Preservation Trust, but mainly, to visitors, it is the General Store, where one can buy artisan goods, books and a cold drink on a hot summer's day.

The village of today: Elizabeth C. White Reception Hall. *Credit Rose McDonald.*

This page and opposite: Whitesbog Village General Store, operated by Whitesbog Preservation Trust, February 4, 2024. *Author's collection.*

Norma T. Vivian Curriculum Center

The center was renamed in 1972, after the first few years of the CESC's operation, to honor Dr. V. Eugene Vivian's late wife Norma T. Vivian. The heart of the village focused on curriculum development.

CESC-produced publications on various topics included: *The Jersey Devil* (1968), *Exploitation of the Pine Barrens* (1969), *Water: The Waste of Plenty* (1969), *Map and Compass Study* (1969), *Angling for an Unknown Dimension* (1969), *Cemeteries and Environments: A Humanistic Approach* (1974).

Norma Vivian passed away at Whitesbog Village while taking a horseback riding skill course; she had suffered from angina prior but was given a positive report from the University of Pennsylvania Hospital. Norma was a Pine Barrens bardess whom history forgot: a public amnesia ushered on by a life cut way too short. She had the fortitude to find the words to preserve and promote the history and folklore of the Pinelands. Her dying, in part, has become Pine Barrens folklore.

The 2024 *Fall Program Guide for Ocean County Parks & Recreation* describes a scheduled activity called "Jaunt to Reevestown Cemetery." The story of Norma's last resting place, where her ashes were spread, takes you through two old towns of the Pines: Whitesbog Village and Warren Grove, home of Reevestown Cemetery. The part of the legend that many believe to

Above: The village of today: Norma T. Vivian Curriculum Center. *Credit Dennis McDonald*.

Right: Logo of the Conservation & Environmental Studies Center Inc. *Author's collection.*

Above: Gravestone of Norma T. Vivian at Reevestown Cemetery. *Courtesy O'Leary family*.

Left: Dr. Eugene Vivian kneeling at his second wife's headstone at the Reevestown Cemetery. *Courtesy O'Leary family*.

Above: Visit to Reevestown Cemetery. *Left to right*: Dr. Vivian, Ted Gordon, Cathy O'Leary. *Courtesy O'Leary family*.

Opposite: Visit to Reevestown Cemetery. *Left to right*: Dr. Vivian and Terry O'Leary. *Courtesy O'Leary family*.

be true says Dr. Vivian spread Norma's ashes in one of Elizabeth White's gardens at Suningive in 1972 and he had a large South Jersey sandstone rock with a bronze plaque memorial installed for his beloved second wife. The legend only grows and turns part folklore when it comes to how the sandstone memorial was moved from Whitesbog to Reevestown Cemetery, more locally known as the Oak Grove Cemetery.

Local tradition says Dr. Vivian left Whitesbog in 1984, never to return, and he and his third wife, Marie, and Terry O'Leary somehow managed to lift the heavy piece of sandstone into a car and relocated it, with permission, to the exclusive cemetery in Warren Grove. One of the stipulations when considering this cemetery as a place to be buried was that membership was limited to people from those few towns in the Pines area. This is an interesting historic cemetery, and Ocean County Parks and Recreation, along with the staff of Cedar Bridge Tavern, offers an annual guided hike through the woods between Cedar Bridge Tavern and Reevestown Cemetery. It's been said that Dr. Vivian believed Norma would have liked to be buried there and that they asked for permission from the onetime mayor of Stafford Township Jack Cervetto (1908–1995), who is now buried at the Reevestown Cemetery. Jack showed Doc the place to put the sandstone: in a corner near a pine tree and a patch of mountain laurel.

The J.W. Harshberger Building

From Wikipedia: "John William Harshberger (January 1, 1869–April 27, 1929) was an American botanist who specialized in plant geography, ecology and plant pathology. He taught at the University of Pennsylvania for more than 35 years. He was an ardent plant conservationist, and he is credited with coining the term *ethnobotany*."

The village of today: J.W. Harshberger building. *Credit Dennis McDonald.*

The village of today: Louis E. Hand Hall. *Credit Dennis McDonald.*

The Louis E. Hand Hall

Louis E. Hand Hall was named for a prominent professor at Cornell University in New York. Not just any professor, Hand served for more than forty years there and is best known as a pioneer of high-energy physics. He died in 2023.

Chapter 8

DR. VIVIAN'S ACES CONSULTING BUSINESS (1984–2001)

THE 1980S: END OF AN ERA

In the 1970s, out of necessity and a love of the out-of-doors, Dr. Vivian, a.k.a. Doc, diversified the offerings at Whitesbog Village through the Conservation and Environmental Studies Center (CESC). Federal dollars had all but dried up, so Doc had to find other ways to fund the ongoing work of educating both children and adults in EE at the center. Throughout the years, many schools would pay to bring their children to the center, but in the 1980s, school budgets started to tighten even more than before. One way to help sustain the center's mission was to take to the field. Leading up to the preservation of the New Jersey Pinelands National Reserve, there was a good amount of environmental casework compiled by very competent people and groups locally so that future experts had access and document research findings in the field for various government regulatory entities. This work was something Doc enjoyed the most, as did many of his former students, in a place full of magical landscapes: the New Jersey Pinelands National Reserve. One didn't need much incentive to go outside and spend long periods in a place that the world came to see as a critically important environment. From NJ.gov: "The Biosphere was originally designated by the United Nations Educational, Scientific and Cultural Organization (or UNESCO) as part of the Man and Biosphere Programme (or MAB) in 1983. At that time, it was part of a multiple-site reserve called the 'South Atlantic Coastal Plain Biosphere Reserve/Pinelands National Reserve."

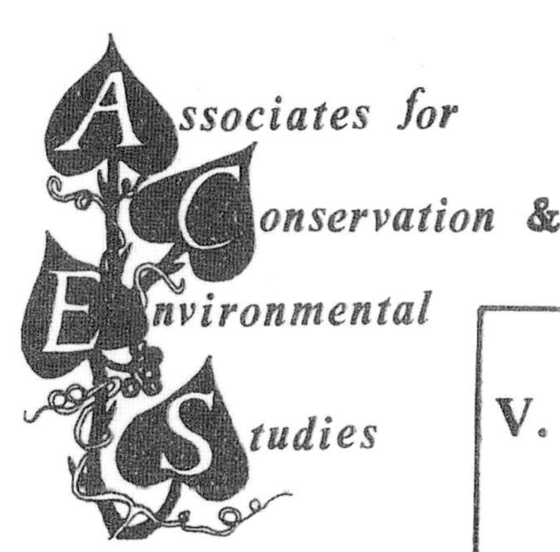

(609) 296-7479

284 COUNTRY CLUB BLVD.
TUCKERTON, N.J. 08087

V. EUGENE VIVIAN, Ph.D.
DIRECTOR

ENVIRONMENTAL PLANNING, ASSESSMENTS, INVENTORIES & IMPACT STATEMENTS

Dr. V. Eugene Vivian's ACES business card. *Courtesy O'Leary family.*

Dr. Vivian would mirror the approach of Lloyd Burgess Sharp (1895–1963), executive director of Life Camps and iconic founding father of resident outdoor education/camp program development, using gained wisdom and expertise to earn money as a consultant, always with an end goal for the benefit of nature in mind. L.B. Sharp struggled alongside Dr. Vivian in his lifetime to acquire enough funds to support outdoor education camps for children and turned to consultant work, where he would survey and develop outdoor camping programs for private (paying) entities like churches and schools. Dr. Vivian took on paid consulting projects as well to help sustain the environmental education program already taking place at Whitesbog Village under the auspices of the CESC Inc. (See Appendix C for a list of environmental consultancies conducted by Dr. Vivian during this period.)

Not all Doc's work was income related, as most teachers can relate to a life of work that is a life of passion. Very knowledgeable about the New Jersey Pine Barrens, with a master's in botany and in the right place at the right time, Doc was sought out for various projects to protect and preserve the New Jersey Pinelands. In the early 1980s, there was a federal project taking place with a team canvassing the communities of the then newly established Pinelands National Reserve. The American Folklife Center at the Library of Congress spearheaded a "culture conservation" effort initiated by Congress, a three-phased plan carried out between 1983 and 1986. The Pinelands Folklife Project (PFP) generated two publications: an official report to Congress, *One Space, Many Places*, by Mary Hufford (1986), and *Pinelands Folklife*, edited by Rita Zorn Moonsammy, David Steven Cohen and Lorraine E. Williams (Rutgers State University, 1987). Professional botanist and ecologist Jim Stasz of Audubon, New Jersey, recommended that Eugene S. Hunn call on Dr. Eugene Vivian at Whitesbog Environmental Center for help with a project he was working on. Hunn's project, focused on Pineland interpretive ethnobiology, was part of the American Folklife Center's effort to capture the Pinelands' existing culture and traditions in order to aid planners as the Pinelands National Reserve evolved. Hunn was a paid participant in the project as an ethnobiology consultant from the University of Washington.

Thankfully, today, one can visit the Library of Congress on the Internet and read through typed-out transcripts of handwritten notes, listen to countless interviews and browse through hundreds of images taken as part of the Pinelands Folklife Project. We know Hunn met Dr. Vivian for the first time on December 19, 1983. At the time, Doc was leading the CESC in Whitesbog Village and performing a lot of fieldwork for independent site surveys. At that first meeting in Doc's office, Hunn and Dr. Vivian spoke for over an hour about the mission of the CESC, and Doc promised to help identify plants of the Pine Barrens, which Hunn, as an ethnobiologist, was documenting and, in some cases, needed local expertise to correctly identify. On that day in 1983, Hunn recorded in his notes a synopsis of what the CESC's mission was:

> *Is self-supporting on fees charged their clientele, mostly schools, youth groups, and some adult groups and private students. His effort is like that of Carl Anderson at Rancocas Nature Center, though Rancocas gets an Audubon Society subsidy: also like Betty Woodford's project, but more stress on longer-term classes, as in his "Pine Barrens Through the Year" class.*

Hunn visited Dr. Vivian numerous times for aid in identifying flora and fauna of the Pinelands Reserve that he encountered during his four short field trips to the area. The results of three years of research conducted by Hunn and his colleagues are archived by the Library of Congress. The resulting publications and interactions between the American Folklife Center's team and other entities in the Pinelands, like the CESC, helped shape the Pinelands of today.

In 1984, Dr. Vivian founded ACES Environmental (Associates for Conservation and Environmental Studies), which he led until his retirement

Circa 2000s photo of Dr. Vivian being recognized at a Little Egg Harbor Environmental Commission event. *Courtesy O'Leary family*.

in 2001. Doc's lease, signed back on February 1, 1969, with the State of New Jersey for village acreage and use of buildings establishing the Conservation and Environmental Studies Center (CESC), officially ended on Tuesday, February 1, 1994. The baton for the center at Whitesbog Village was passed to successor and fellow professor Gary Patterson, in conjunction with his position at Glassboro State College. Doc, in an interview with *Press of Atlantic City* staff writer Michael McGarry, said of his reasons for retirement, "I was working like Sam Hill to keep (the center going). Everybody said, 'You're working too hard, you better stop.'" And he did not go into a stereotypical retirement where his days were spent idly sipping lemonade and people-watching at the beach. ACES Environmental kept Doc teaching and inspiring others as he had done at Glassboro State College and the CESC.

While Doc was a consultant for the Manahawkin Environmental Commission, a project was started and aided by Doc's expertise and experience with the Southern Regional High School Environmental Club students that, on completion, received the April 1999 President's Youth Environmental Award from the U.S. Environmental Protection Agency. The project took place at Oxycocus Bogs, Forsythe National Wildlife Refuge and entailed "managing a quaking bog habitat for globally rare plants."

In the *Tuckerton Beacon*, on January 20, 2000, J.P. White reported, "Vivian said he hopes his work is not in vain. 'We're in serious trouble,' he said. Because of overpopulation, Vivian said, New Jersey is under developmental pressure. 'We're fragmenting our open areas—biting a piece out here and there.'" Yet Doc continued to battle on. Ever the optimist, he continued to advocate for the environment and for people to see a place for themselves in the environment as good stewards. And he continued to seek out other environmentally minded teachers to plant the seeds of tomorrow's guardian acorn trees.

Several colleagues had these words to say about ACES under Doc's leadership:

> *We had to do a job, Doc and I. He was a stick to the ground. An example: we had to do a job at the nuclear power plant. The instance was they wanted to build a development right next to the power plant. So they sent their environmental consultant from the power plant where we met them in the woods. We take them out there, and we tell them that if you lift a piece of lumber, you might find a snake under it.*
>
> *And right there, the only place you could cross the wetlands to get there, there's a pine snake, a four-foot pine snake. I picked up the pine snake and*

Doc Vivian and employee Terry O'Leary working a consultant job measuring a live pine snake. *Courtesy O'Leary family.*

> *asked if the guy wanted to hold it. And he had never held one before. I took his picture holding the snake with the stack of the power plant in the background. Later, we got a call from the guy's boss saying we'd never get paid if we didn't destroy that picture. We didn't care if we were going to get paid; we couldn't be bought. You pay for the facts. Good news or bad news. You might think it's bad news, but we might think it's good news. Stick to your guns and do the right thing.*
>
> *Doc and I used to meet in the center of the state. He was coming from Tuckerton, and I was coming from Bayville to meet him at Marshal's Corner in New Egypt, New Jersey, to go out and do fieldwork. We'd have breakfast before we went out.*
>
> *—Terry O'Leary, age seventy-six, personal communication, January 30, 2024*

Cathy O'Leary, Terry's wife, says, "I'd get a call from the police because they were out on this property and found these two guys with headlamps

Above: Doc Vivian and Terry O'Leary enjoying an end of the workday drink out in the Pines. *Courtesy O'Leary family*.

Left: Terry O'Leary showing the gentleness of a pine snake. *Courtesy O'Leary family*.

on, waiting for treefrogs to call. Trying to convince a cop of that is pretty funny and hard to do." They were in Galloway by the refuge, Terry later told his wife.

> *The time I was working with him was with Bob Zappalorti with the herps (herpetologists use this term to describe searching for amphibians and reptiles), and the plant guy was Terry O'Leary. I was doing bird work, in the early '90s to mid-'90s, four or five years. When I started teaching at Pinelands, I was also teaching at Ocean County College at night in their nursing program (chemistry). And I was coaching two different sports. With Doc, it wasn't an everyday thing anyway; he'd call me up when he had a job for me. A lot of it was sand and quarry pits. And I'd go out looking for barred owls and such. It was a lot of fun, interesting work. Over the years I found barred owls and red-headed woodpeckers, either endangered or threatened species. I submitted what I found to Doc. I never questioned Doc's integrity; he had a great reputation. When he was at Glassboro, he was a professor emeritus there. No one had anything bad to say about him. I just figured he was a straight shooter.*
>
> *—Joe Palumbo, retired teacher, age seventy-seven, personal communication, January 29, 2024*

> *Somebody referred me to Doc, which was a retirement job for him. I worked part time for him, for a little less than two years, 1988–89. It was a wonderful experience. Once an educator, always an educator. He always took the time to explain things. Part of what we were doing involved identifying plants at a site. We were doing wetland delineations based on the regulations. Developers can't build in the wetlands. One of the ways you determined if the spot was wetlands or not was the vegetation. He knew what everything was, but he would not just make a list and I would take notes. He would tell me how he knew what each plant was and how to identify it. You could just tell he still had that love of teaching. It was usually the two of us doing this. If you were doing an endangered species search, you have to determine before an area was developed.*
>
> *He was very professional as far as following all the environmental rules. There might have been another environmental consultant here and there that was a little less ethical. Maybe there were five acres of wetlands on a site, and they would say there were two so the developer got the number of units they wanted to build. That was not Dr. Vivian. This was a retirement job for him, and he was going to maintain his integrity. Whatever the situation*

on the ground was, whether it was the amount of wetland or the presence of endangered species, that's the information that was recorded and given to the developer that he was hired by. I learned a lot about integrity as well as the environment, identifying the varying species. Somebody had to enforce the rules or at least follow the rules. It became apparent that Dr. Vivian believed that, too. It was his integrity in following the laws that dictated why he was doing what he was doing.

—German Georgieff, current Ocean County chief park naturalist, age sixty-three, personal communication, January 26, 2024

Chapter 9

NURSERIES OF ENVIRONMENTAL EDUCATION

Acorns to Mighty Oaks

The questions to be decided here are the ones implied by the two definitions of nature. Is man to be understood as standing over against or as in the environment? Is the basic stress to be on dependence or independence, or possibly, interdependence? Is man so little lower than the angels that the natural order is to be a secondary consolidation at best, or is he of the dust and therefore inextricably tied to the rest of creation?

—*From the 1970 book* Crisis in Eden, *by Frederick Elder*

In alphabetical order on the following pages are nurseries for the environmental education movement in New Jersey. Not all of them, mind you. As this list was fastidiously being filled out, there was one requirement: that the entity be influenced by Dr. V. Eugene Vivian or one of his oak saplings, of which he planted the acorn so many years ago. We apologize if the reader has never read either of J.R.R. Tolkien's seminal works, *The Hobbit* and or *The Lord of the Rings*; nevertheless, a Tolkien reference is appropriate here. After the CESC center closed, it might have felt to some like Rivendell, the last elven sanctuary on Middle-earth, a place of peace and exquisite beauty existing in nature, not built on or above nature but interlaced with it, had fallen and the only way home for the remaining elves was to take a ship and sail to Valinor. Those who worked with Doc may have had the realization that their part in the EE movement had come to an end. But the environmental ethic and teacher's consciousness don't allow it to end.

Dr. Vivian wrote in his seminal work *Sourcebook for Environmental Education* (1973), "Environmental Education has the unique potential not only to rejuvenate children's desire to learn directly, but also to produce a generation of youngsters disposed toward continued involvement with societal progress." Many of those youngsters, before they knew what "the environment" even meant, were bitten by the curiosity bug, motivating them onward to learn and to one day teach, which can lead to a lifetime of learning. And one of the first books about teaching in the environment was by the teacher and author L.H. Bailey, in 1903. Bailey wrote, "When teacher is full of the subject, he cannot help teaching."

In a place like New Jersey, home to the nation's first national reserve, the New Jersey Pinelands National Reserve, nature exhibits abound, and the duty to teach is infused with as much magic as an elven cloak of Rivendell and or the responsibility of ethically supporting the oak saplings of tomorrow. Dr. Vivian and his acorn saplings had a far-reaching and caring hand in South Jersey. In the Pines, as they say, one is immersed in a classroom that teaches all day and all night about the wonders of nature. During the time spent in this laboratory or library of nature, one can't help but want to learn everything there is to know, to protect and to teach with the same amazement and wonder that inspired the curious child to become a teacher.

The history of the goings-on in these environmental education strongholds should be important to all of us, not just those in the EE field. It's during time spent away from a space and place that we begin to forget the memories made there. And the space and place all but forget who and what we did there. Whether we've gone away for a little while or are dead to the earth, the historical events we participated in are part of the landscape's history. Unknowingly, it's the next generation's duty to remember history and pick up where we left off. A historian or a teacher can help tomorrow's generation remember and learn from the past life.

Each of us spends hours, days, months and a lifetime of toil on and in the brown soil. If at a young age we're not introduced to our duty and responsibility to the earth, we aimlessly move about the globe not caring or seeing the world in all its glory—like a person who wears glasses and has lost them. The outline of the trees can be seen, and the varying shades of green are apparent, but the vast beauty and the freely given life lessons contained within the smallest of details in the woods are lost to those uninitiated. The villainous act or antagonist in this story is that the teacher did not get to open the eyes of the student. Doc spent a lifetime teaching adults to teach about the environment surrounding the child, the caretakers of our collective future. He cherished teaching children the most, as most of the people involved in the "tree nurseries" described in this chapter do, too. "But the greatest reward," Doc said (as quoted in *New Jersey Outdoors* in July/August 1975), "is seeing the expressions on children's faces when they directly discover something new about the environment in which they reside."

Each and every one of these institutions, their staff and volunteers ask the question Doc posed: "What can education do for failing environments?"

Barnegat Bay Decoy and Baymen's Museum (now Tuckerton Seaport)

Category: Nonprofit
Website: https://tuckertonseaport.org

Years of the community's need to preserve the Baymen's way of life cumulated, finally, residing under one roof in Tuckerton, New Jersey. Bob Birdsall's 2007 book *People of the Pines* outlines that destined feat involving a pupil of Dr. Vivian's, "When some of [Terry O'Leary's] former students became involved with the fledgling Baymen's Museum, they called on their mentor, who subsequently became program director, publicist, grant-writer, and jack-of-all-trades to what would ultimately become the Tuckerton Seaport Museum." Today the museum offers ferry rides, traditional craft demonstrations and historical tours.

Mike Magnum, in 2024, said,

> *At the first show (Old Time Barnegat Bay Decoy and Gunning Show), Sam Hunt was set up with his hand-crafted rustic furniture, sneakboxes, and banjos. Merce Ridgeway and some other musicians from the Pinelands Cultural Society sat in Sammy's chairs and started playing music with him, and the impromptu act from these legends of Barnegat Bay started the tradition of having music at the show.*

Camp Pioneer

Category: Nonprofit
Website: https://freshair.org

In the *Tuckerton Beacon*, on January 20, 2000, J.P. White wrote,

> *Camp Pioneer, the first camp established on the reservation, was for disadvantaged boys ages 12 to 14. Vivian also served as director of camping and research for the Fresh Air Fund in 1951. "There was nothing*

there but woods," said Vivian, who was responsible for getting a swimming pool and tent camps built on the reservation.

In Doc's honor, that year, on the projected 2002 completion of an updated Fresh Air Fund Director's Office, the building would be renamed the Eugene Vivian Director's Office. A special note in 2000 about the Fresh Air Fund, as reported in the *Tuckerton Beacon*: "An independent, not-for-profit agency, the fund has provided free two-week summer vacation for more than 1.6 million disadvantaged New York City children since 1877."

Camp Pioneer was renamed Camp Tommy in honor of a large donation by fashion designer and cultural icon Tommy Hilfiger.

Cedar Run Wildlife Refuge

Category: Nonprofit
Website: https://www.cedarrun.org

Two mighty oaks inspired by their surroundings: Elizabeth "Betty" Woodford and her husband, James Woodford, built their dream house in Medford Township in 1957. The project eventually morphed into a state-renowned rehabilitation center for injured wildlife and also a haven for environmental education. James was a formal educator; Betty herself became known as an expert botanist teaching programs on the Pinelands. In *People of the Pines*, Bob Birdsall wrote, "Betty taught Pinelands ecology courses at Lenape evening school and many of her students, including Ted Gordon, went on to become noted environmentalists." Their daughter Jeanne Woodford, once an elementary and special education teacher in Moorestown, New Jersey, has solidified their legacy by partnering with the New Jersey State Green Acres program in preserving the land, which has added to their conservation efforts and continued their critical mission since being incorporated, in 1981, as a nonprofit.

Jeanne Woodford of Cedar Run Wildlife Refuge and author William J. Lewis in Medford, New Jersey, at Autumn with the Animals annual fall event, September 22, 2024. *Author's collection.*

Cedar Run Wildlife Refuge's mission statement is as follows:

> *Cedar Run is a non-profit dedicated to the preservation of New Jersey's wildlife and habitats through education, conservation and rehabilitation. How we achieve this... Woodford Cedar Run Wildlife Refuge sits on 171 wooded acres on the edge of the New Jersey Pinelands. Cedar Run includes the Woodford Nature Center, an outdoor Wildlife Housing Area with nearly 60 native residents, and a Wildlife Rehabilitation Hospital. The overall mission of Cedar Run is to serve as a community resource on the importance of protecting and enhancing healthy ecosystems for all.*

It would be an injustice to Elizabeth M. Woodford's life if the reader was not made aware of her prose that professed an adoring love of the environment, especially the New Jersey Pine Barrens. In an article titled "Summer in the New Jersey Pine Barrens," published in the July 1968 issue of *Horticulture* magazine, Woodford wrote about the Pine Barrens,

> *Its most striking quality is how "unbarren" the Barrens really are. However, conservation in the Pine Barrens is essential. I believe that in order to develop a wish to conserve, something must first be proved special. Plans have been made to set aside forever a portion of the Pine Barrens as a national preserve. Support for this action will be strongest from those who get to know the Pine Barrens for what they mean as a precious resource.*

Cherry Hill Environmental Education Residency (CHEER) Program on Pinelands Ecology

Category: Education

Website: https://www.chclc.org

This environmental education program has been discontinued; it stopped just before the COVID-19 pandemic began, and a scaled-down version now takes place at the YMCA, with no overnight residency included. Once the sixth grade Mount Misery Environmental Residency Program, it included an annual trip for all incoming sixth graders from John A. Carusi Middle School as part of the Cherry Hill Environmental Education Curriculum. Each house spent four days and three nights at the campsite, leaving from and returning to Carusi.

Here are experiences shared by two former students:

> *At all Cherry Hill schools back then, in the early 1990s, in the sixth grade, you would go to Mount Misery Monday to Friday. I went to Joyce Kilmer Elementary School, and most schools were coed. It was a big deal because it was significant when sixth grade was done and you were graduating from elementary school heading into middle school, kind of symbolizing that you were growing up and getting mature. At that time, there were Joyce Kilmer and Clara Barton Elementary School, Cherry Hill East and West—we all went to Mount Misery. It was a great experience that lets you have that bond with those who are in your class and are graduating with you. And the teachers got to go with you. Cabins were assigned, where there were bunk beds, and each of us brought our sleeping bags. There was a shower in each cabin. And there was a designated area where we could eat together.*
>
> *The whole experience at age eleven picking through the nature of Mount Misery and learning the history of the place. They also taught us survival skills. I remember there were six of us, and we were dropped off with a compass. We had to find our way back using a map. For a lot of us, it was the first time being out in the woods. That was the first time for most of us, as we were mostly suburban kids. We mostly hung out at the bowling lane or the Cherry Hill Mall. Every day, there was something for us to do. A lot of walking, and learning about different trees, plants and flowers. I remember teachers telling us ghost stories around a campfire. A lot of kids are used to technology. They don't read books—it's Chromebooks. And they don't go for a walk in the woods with their kids; it's not part of our daily lives. It's a different culture now; we don't do that. Honestly, they do Facebooking—and soccer no more on the front lawn or backyard playing. I think preserving nature is important. The Pinelands are a known place in New Jersey, and it's important for people to be connected to nature. Again, Mother Nature is important. And it's important to know certain survival skills. It's also important to take care of nature as well, like not polluting nature.*
>
> *—Helen Son, age forty-three, Cherry Hill school graduate, personal communication, March 18, 2024*

> *My class field trip to Mount Misery was one of the most memorable school trips I ever had. I remember it vividly to this day: learning about the Pine Barrens and the aquifer while doing team-building exercises to deepen my friendships with others. It gave me a deep appreciation for the nature we are caretakers and stewards for and how we benefit from preserving and*

maintaining the world around us. And of course, I think I still have my "I Survived Mount Misery" T-shirt somewhere in my home.

—Senator Andy Kim, age forty-two, Cherry Hill Public Schools at James F. Cooper Elementary School, personal communication, November 16, 2024

Citizens Conservation Council of Ocean County

Category: Unincorporated nonprofit
Website: Dissolved

Contributing editor of this work Janet Larson, now retired from Rutgers Cooperative Extension of Ocean County, recalls,

> *Citizens Conservation Council of Ocean County was an organization formed during the early years of the environmental movement as a coalition of dozens of environmental groups. Robert (Bob) Anstett, a bread truck driver from Brick, New Jersey, was the driving force. He also served on the advisory committee of Save Barnegat Bay and on the board of trustees of Clean Ocean Action. Bob believed people would be moved to action if they knew what was being eroded away in their communities.*
>
> *As the years passed, he was one of the first activists to turn to the preforming arts as a method of teaching environmental protection. Some of the stewardship techniques promoted were art contests for schoolchildren, poetry writing and readings and plays, all themed around environmental protection. The organization dissolved upon Bob's death, but the Township of Brick recognized his accomplishments by naming the Robert Anstett Cultural Arts Center in his honor.*
>
> *—Information provided by Janet Newbury Larson, age seventy-seven, and Gene Donatiello, age eighty-six, Brick Historical Society, September 15, 2024*

Federation of Conservationists United Societies (FOCUS)

Category: Nonprofit
Website: Dissolved

Groups like the Pine Barrens Coalition and FOCUS, the Federation of Conservationists United Societies, coalesced around the environmental movement in the latter half of the twentieth century. FOCUS predated the Pine Barrens Coalition but faced the same challenges in engaging, educating and evolving the public's earthly consciousness. Reporting for the *Ocean County Reporter* in an award-winning ten-part series of articles about the Pine Barrens (1969–75), Lee M. Gant Thorn writes, "Cooper [A. Morton Cooper of Toms River], president of the Conservationists United Societies (FOCUS) along with a host of conservation-minded people, has been working for several years to protect and preserve sections of the Pinelands for future generations to enjoy."

Before there was the Pinelands National Reserve in 1978, ecowarriors were fighting to "protect and preserve" what today is protected and nearly 25 percent of the acreage of New Jersey: the Pinelands. This was the important work of environmentalists Elizabeth "Betty" D. Newbury Cooper, née Newbury (1907–1991) and Eagle Scout A. Morton Cooper (1902–1985) of Toms River: educating star reporters like Lee M. Gant Thorn, thus allowing her writing to influence and educate the public at large. Thorn also wrote in the *Reporter* series, "There are many groups in South Jersey interested in the Pine Barrens area. Many conservation societies have sprung up, and one group, the Federation of Conservationists United Societies (FOCUS), is extremely active." Betty Cooper was a teacher and librarian: the network of teachers almost never ends.

A bit more of the history of the organization from personal communication with Janet Newbury Larson:

> *FOCUS was an organization headed up by several dedicated individuals, including the Walnut Family. A. Jerome Walnut (Jerry) lived on LBI (Barnegat Light) and was on the Ocean County Soil Conservation District Board of Supervisors and the Ocean County Board of Agriculture. He was also chairperson of the Ocean County Environmental Agency following Mort Cooper. He worked for Burlington County in their Planning Department as a cartographer before retirement. His brother and sister-in-law, Rick and Nan Walnut (lived in South Hampton Township, Burlington County), plus several others, were movers and shakers in FOCUS. Nan was a very strong advocate for Pinelands protection, later helping to establish the Pine Barrens Coalition.*

The Forked River Mountain Coalition

Category: Nonprofit
Website: http://www.frmc.org

This group was founded by trustees of the Forked Mountain Coalition: "Pines Baroness" Elizabeth Morgan, Terry O'Leary, Ted Gordon, Gladys Eayre and Janice Sherwood. The last two, Gladys and Janice, were key members of the popular Pine Barrens band the Pineconers.

From the website Forked River Mountain Coalition:

> *The Forked River Mountain Coalition is a grass-roots organization working to conserve, maintain, protect, and restore the natural, cultural, historical, recreational, and other resources of the Forked River Mountains. The Forked River Mountain Coalition is a charitable, nonprofit 501(c)(3) organization; contributions are tax deductible.*
>
> *P.O. Box 219*
> *Forked River, New Jersey 08731*

On top of Forked River Mountain, the Pineconers sing. *Left to right*: John Krauthause, a.k.a. Mr. Spoons; Gladys Eayre; and Janice Sherwood. *Courtesy O'Leary family*.

Opposite: Circa 1990s view from top of Forked River Mountain. *Courtesy O'Leary family.*

Above: Circa 1990s image of children taking a footpath up to the top of Forked River Mountain. *Courtesy O'Leary family.*

Friends of Whitesbog

Category: N/A

Website: https://www.facebook.com/groups/150079525528683

In the July/August 1975 issue of *New Jersey Outdoors*, reporter Thomas H. Griffin Jr. wrote,

> *The Friends of Whitesbog, a service arm of CESC, is also offering monthly presentations and field trips to members and guests interested in the restoration of a company town and exploring the Pinelands. These monthly meetings have met with continued success and currently include canoe trips, excellent slide presentations by members and friends, a hunting workshop, and an old-fashioned square dance.*

Friends of Whitesbog was an organization to help keep CESC afloat. In the same article, Doc outlines the reasons why the fight is worth fighting:

> *Environmental problems should be viewed in a truly ecological manner; considering not only the natural world but politics, economics, ethics, and all other disciplines. Search for alternatives and study the problem profusely before making decisions that might alter the lives of present and future generations. The sad fact is that environmental knowledge and environmental awareness don't always lead to environmental wisdom. This can only come after a critical analysis of each situation.*

Today the Friends of Whitesbog group is helping spread the good word of what Whitesbog Village is all about.

Glassboro State College (now Rowan University, since 1997)

Category: Institution of higher education
Website: https://www.rowan.edu

Historical background of what is known today as Rowan University and was in Dr. V. Eugene Vivian's time known as Glassboro State College (it was one of the newest normal schools):

> *The State Teachers College at Glassboro, New Jersey, was inaugurated as a Normal School in 1923. Under the guidance of Dr. J.J. Savitz, this institution offered two years of academic and laboratory training to prospective teachers. To comply with the state requirements, the two-year course has evolved into a more extensive and intensive four-year course, and the status of the institution has been changed from a State Normal School to a State Teachers College. The first change occurred in 1929. At this time, the two-year course was extended to three. The present four-year course was instituted in 1935.*

Active cranberry harvest at Whitesbog Village in September.

As the bog's water level lowers, spring migratory birds come to Whitesbog Village.

Young couple on a dike separating bogs at Whitesbog Village.

Bearberry, *Arctostaphylos uva-ursi*.

Black huckleberry, *Gaylussacia baccata*.

Blazing star, *Liatris pilosa*.

Cow-wheat, *Melampyrum lineare*.

Cranberry, *Vaccinium macrocarpon*.

Left: Dangleberry, *Gaylussacia frondosa*.

Below: Fragrant water lily, *Nymphaea odorata*.

Above: Golden club, *Orontium aquaticum*.

Left: Indian Pipe, *Monotropa uniflora*.

Right: Horsemint, *Monarda punctata*.

Below: Highbush blueberry, *Vaccinium corymbosum*.

Above: Leatherleaf, *Chamaedaphne calyculata*.

Left: Maryland golden aster, *Chrysopsis mariana*.

Above: Nodding lady's tresses, *Spiranthes cernua*.

Right: White heath heather, *Symphyotrichum ericoides*.

Above: Orange milkwort, *Polygala lutea*.

Left: Pink lady's slipper, *Cypripedium acaule*.

Above: Purple pitcher plant, *Sarracenia purpurea*.

Right: Rose pogonia, *Pogonia ophioglossoides*.

Above: Sheep laurel, *Kalmia angustifolia*.

Left: Stiff-leaved aster, *Ionactis linariifolius*.

Above: Swamp azalea, *Rhododendron viscosum*.

Right: Swamp candles, *Lysimachia terrestris*.

Above: Sweet pepperbush, *Clethra alnifolia*.

Left: Tawny cotton grass, *Eriophorum virginicum*.

Left: Threadleaf gerardia, *Agalinis setacea*.

Below: Teaberry, *Gaultheria procumbens*.

Top: Turkeybeard, *Xerophyllum asphodeloides*.

Bottom: Turk's-cap lily, *Lilium superbum*.

When the school became a Teachers College offering a Bachelor of Science degree in Elementary Education to its graduates, Dr. Edgar F. Bunce, President of the Glassboro State Teachers College since Dr. Savitz's retirement in 1936, was the State Supervisor of Teacher Training. In the latter capacity, he was instrumental in changing the state requirements from three years of training to four.

Little Egg Harbor Township Environmental Commission

Category: Government (state)
Website: https://www.leht.com/environmental-commission

An excerpt from the commission's web page follows.

A volunteer organization sponsored by taxpayer dollars centered on the environment as the main focus. Asbury Park Press *article "Pine Barrens Scientist, Educator Dies at 93" discusses Dr. Vivian's time with the LEHT Environmental Commission: "He remained active in the environmental affairs, working as a consultant, educator, and chairman of the Little Egg Harbor Township Environmental Commission, where he also started the township's recycling program." Doc had moved to LEH in 1976.*

Vision Statement

The Little Egg Harbor Environmental Commission is comprised of community volunteers that are passionate about improving the quality of life for our residents by protecting our unique environment, educating the youth and community on sustainable habits and different ecosystems, along with supporting all activities in the community that impact protection, use, and restoration of natural resources and open space.

Accomplishments:

- *Little Egg Harbor Township has achieved Bronze Status with Sustainable Jersey. This is awarded to municipalities who fulfill environmentally friendly goals in a given year.*
- *Conducting town wide clean-ups*
- *Held 1st Green Fair*
- *Terrapin awareness poster contest with 2nd grade students*
- *Present Environmental Hero award yearly*

MARINE ACADEMY OF TECHNOLOGY AND ENVIRONMENTAL SCIENCE (MATES)
Category: Nonprofit
Website: https://www.matesocvts.org

This organization has been operating since 1990. From the "About Us" section of the Marine Academy of Technology and Environmental Science (MATES) Ocean County Vocational Technical School (OCVTS) website:

> *The Marine Academy of Technology and Environmental Science provides an enriched STEM learning environment that has helped countless students learn, develop and grow. Our unparalleled curriculum and teaching methods help students take the next step in their education and approach the future with confidence and the ability to critically think.*
>
> *We have the privilege of teaching bright and curious students throughout Ocean County, NJ. Our curriculum offers experiential learning and community-based projects. We have a multitude of partners in the STEAM fields that support student learning experiences. We are a program of the Ocean County Vocational Technical School, which supports real-world applications. Our slogan is "Barnegat Bay Is Our Classroom."*

NATURAL RESOURCE EDUCATION FOUNDATION IN WARETOWN
Category: Nonprofit
Website: https://lighthousecenternj.org

From the Lighthouse Center website:

> *The Natural Resources Education Foundation (NREF) of New Jersey provides immersive educational experiences for all ages at the Lighthouse Center for Environmental Education in Waretown, NJ.*
>
> *NREF serves as the steward of the Lighthouse Center Property which is owned by the New Jersey Department of Environmental Protection. Located on Barnegat Bay this site serves as our natural laboratory as we work to understand and manage this coastal gem in the face of climate change.*

The ninety-four-acre piece of land and all the buildings were first purchased by the Trust for Public Land in September 2000 from New York–based Lighthouse Inc. At one time, it was a camp for the blind, which Lighthouse Inc. ran from 1926 to 1996. It was an important place

Elizabeth Morgan Inspirational Garden at Natural Resources Education Foundation (NREF) in Waretown, New Jersey. *Courtesy the O'Leary family.*

that was saved from being developed by many people in the environmental community. A sampling of those people: Terry O'Leary, Elizabeth Morgan (an Inspirational Garden dedicated to Elizabeth Morgan resides today at the site), Governor Christine Todd Whitman, Cathy O'Leary, Christine Raabe and many more.

In 1978, Terry O'Leary, William Fulcher and their mentor and boss Dr. Vivian conducted an Environmental Resource Inventory of Ocean Township as part of work done under the roof of the Conservation and Environmental Studies Center in Browns Mills. This covered the Lighthouse Center, which at the time was also in Ocean Township. Both Dr. Vivian and Terry O'Leary were early advocates for the preservation of the property, which they knew intimately. Years later, in 1999, consultants Christine Raabe and Terry O'Leary conducted a feasibility study for the Trust for Public Land 501(c)(3) nonprofit. Another interesting note: this site has connections to the artist community and especially the sounds of the Pine Barrens. Two of the prominent figures in a piney-esque band and their family members at one time lived and helped maintain the site: none other than Pineconers members Gladys Eayre and Janice Sherwood, recognized today as staff emeritus.

New Jersey Conservation Foundation

Category: Nonprofit
Website: https://www.njconservation.org

This nonprofit 501(c)(3) had a lease at Whitesbog Village alongside Dr. Vivian and the CESC in the early 1980s. Their mission statement reads, "The mission of New Jersey Conservation Foundation is to preserve land and natural resources throughout New Jersey for the benefit of all."

For an August 19, 2008 *Asbury Park Press* article, staff writers Kirk Moore and Paula Scully interviewed executive director of the New Jersey Conservation Foundation (NJCF) Michele Byers, who retired in 2021 and who (per Terry O'Leary, in a personal communication) was once an intern at Whitesbog Village under Doc's leadership. Byers said, "He [Doc] truly loved the Pine Barrens and was responsible for introducing tens of thousands of schoolchildren to the beauty and mystery of this wondrous region."

New Jersey Department of Environmental Protection (NJDEP)

Category: Government (state)
Website: https://dep.nj.gov

An environmental force in New Jersey was founded on the same day as the first Earth Day in 1970. From the New Jersey Department of Environmental Protection Agency's website:

> *DEP Mission: Dedicated to improving and protecting public health and the environment we share, NJDEP uses the best available science to guide the conservation of natural and historic resources, ensure a stable climate and resilient communities, and secure clean and healthy air, water and lands throughout New Jersey. Committed to sustainable economic growth, NJDEP invests in communities and infrastructure, provides quality open and recreational spaces for residents and visitors, enforces environmental laws, and furthers the promise of environmental justice for all.*

New Jersey School of Conservation (SOC)

Category: Nonprofit
Website: https://njsoc.org

The New Jersey School of Conservation recently celebrated seventy-five years. From its website: "The mission of the NJSOC is to foster environmental knowledge and action through education programs delivered in a natural setting. We are a community of diverse, responsible stewards of the earth who promote sustainability practices, climate change mitigation and environmental justice."

In a February 2008 founder's group of the New Jersey School of Conservation (SOC) interview with Annette Sambolin, one of the last interviews of Dr. Vivian's life, Doc spoke of the founding of SOC. Doc was there at the beginning of Memorial Day weekend in 1949; at the time, he was a science professor at Paterson State College.

> *The state board of ed decided it would be good to have it mandated that the students of the state colleges (go) to the SOC. They would have aspects of Environmental Education and outdoor education. Outdoor ed meant teaching best in the out of doors what could be best taught there.*

Assistant professor Ed Lee Glassboro State College trip to Stokes and SOC, December 6, 1961. *Courtesy O'Leary family.*

Assistant professor Ed Lee combined Glassboro and Paterson State College field biology trip to SOC, October 3, 1961. *Courtesy O'Leary family.*

Above: Assistant professor Ed Lee combined Glassboro and Paterson State College geology trip to Sunrise Mountain, October 3, 1961. *Courtesy O'Leary family*.

Left: Glassboro and Paterson State College students atop Sunrise Mountain, October 3, 1961. *Courtesy O'Leary family*.

Experience gained at the founding of NJSOC had a profound impact on the teacher Doc would become. And it continues to impact teachers in New Jersey and students of environmental education. As Doc said in the same interview with Annette Sambolin, summarizing the importance of the Stokes State Forest facility, "We have evidence that students learn better and more permanently when they are taking part in these environmental and outdoor education experiences…compared to traditional learning." What better place than Camp Wapalanne and the expanded facilities here in Sussex County, New Jersey?

Ocean County, New Jersey Parks

Category: Government (state)
Website: https://www.oceancountyparks.org
Cattus Island Advisory Council

The council was set up in 1981, according to a February 2011 article on the website Patch by Don Bennett titled, "How Cattus Island Park Came to Be." The article states that a nine-member advisory council appointed by the board of freeholders, today called commissioners, with three alternate members serving without salary or other compensation, has met once a month or every other month since 1981. In 1995, following the advocacy of Dr. Vivian, the county built an observation deck and dedicated it to "Dorothy Hale, a full-time volunteer, who led the volunteer program and served as a park adviser. Other prominent members of the council included protégés of Dr. Vivian: Lois Schoeck (1939–2020) and Christine Raabe." The following information was provided by Janet Newbury Larson, longtime secretary to the council and granddaughter of Betty and Mort Cooper, for whom the Cooper Environmental Center at the Ocean County Cattus Island Park is named, on September 17, 2024.

> *When the park was first developed, it was decided that they wanted to have a panel of experts help them advise them in the managing of it. These were all volunteers who met one evening a month. And it involved at least a half dozen people in various fields of expertise. Both Terry O'Leary and Dr. Vivian were plant experts, but there were other people, perhaps experts in wildlife and other realms of the environment. They advised the chief naturalist, who would then relay that to the parks administration. It was nothing binding, but they would advise on managing the land*

Cooper Environmental Center at Cattus Island County Park. *Author's collection.*

> *itself, vegetation, wildlife populations, the environmental programs, and educational activities that were going on. In some cases, recreation conducts boat tours and, of course, hiking trails. With hiking trails, you have to balance the recreational opportunity for the public to disturbing a minimal amount of the park. Everything would be run by the advisory board and commented on. If we said we were going to do some management activity for endangered species in a certain part of the park, they would give us advice on how to do it or recommend we should be doing it in the first place, as well as criticize anything that they felt harmful.*
>
> *A longtime member of that advisory council, Dr. Eugene Vivian, donated his books to the library in his name.*
>
> *Everyone who is in that field eventually has their own little library that they're looking to donate to. The timing was right for Dr. Vivian. The time Cattus Island Park was established was the time Dr. Vivian retired as a college professor and had a good-size library to disperse. It was the perfect timing for Cattus Island to be the recipient of that.*
>
> *—German Georgieff, current Ocean County chief park naturalist, age sixty-three, personal communication, January 26, 2024*

Ocean County, New Jersey Parks

Category: Government (state)
Wells Mills County Park, Waretown, New Jersey
Website: https://www.oceancountyparks.org

The Wells Mills County Park website lists all the activities and facilities available at this county park: "Bike trail, canoe rental (seasonal), conservation area, fishing, handicapped accessible, nature center, open playing fields, picnic area, playground, restrooms." One key feature of the nature center and also a direct tie to Dr. Vivian is the third-floor Elizabeth Meirs Morgan Observation Deck, dedicated in honor of the historian, botanist and friend of the environment. Dr. Vivian wrote in the Elizabeth Meirs Morgan (1913–2004) *In Memoriam* booklet,

> *Elizabeth was always ready and willing to respond to a call for help!... Elizabeth and I were in the habit of telephoning each other whenever we needed special information....* [One] *time I fondly remember is our tramping through the woods in search of the Pine Barrens bellwort—two octogenarians enjoying an outdoor event together.*

Elizabeth Morgan and the Jersey Devil at Wells Mills County Park. *Courtesy O'Leary family.*

Young Elizabeth Morgan and family. *From top left*: Elizabeth Meirs, Helen Gaskill, Sarah Meirs, Anna Meirs Wills, Lucretia Meirs. *Middle row, left to right*: MaryAnn Meirs, Elizabeth Waln Meirs, young Elizabeth Morgan née Meirs (with bow in hair), Ann Weightman Meirs. *Front row, left to right*: John Meirs, John Meirs Jr., Jarvis Meirs. *Courtesy the Meirs family.*

Known to many as the "Pines Baroness," Elizabeth was a mentor and mighty oak to all who encountered her: Dr. Vivian, Terry O'Leary, German Georgieff, Mike Magnum, Lillian Hoey Gomez and the list goes on and on.

Ocean County, New Jersey Parks

Category: Government (state)
Forest Resource Education Center (FREC), Jackson Township
Website: https://www.nj.gov/dep/parksandforests/forest/education/frec.html

In Bob Birdsall's 2007 book *People of the Pines*, Dr. Vivian is listed as an environmental educator and mentor. Similarly, one of Doc's acorns who was a leading force in environmental education at the FREC, Terry O'Leary, was featured in Birdsall's book as an "author and environmental educator." Birdsall writes,

Top: Cathy O'Leary at Forest Resource Education Center (FREC) Jackson Township, New Jersey. *Courtesy O'Leary family*.

Middle: Terry O'Leary at Forest Resource Education Center (FREC) Jackson Township, New Jersey. *Courtesy O'Leary family*.

Bottom: Naturalist Rick Bentz (retired Wharton State Forest superintendent and District Fire Warden for New Jersey Forest Fire Service) with students at Forest Resource Education Center (FREC) Jackson Township, New Jersey. *Courtesy O'Leary family*.

Since 2000 Terry has been the education coordinator and resource interpretive specialist for the Forest Resource Education Center (FREC) in Jackson Township. "I'm a conservationist," he says about teaching that trees are a renewable resource, "but I've never been afraid of cutting trees and managing the forest, particularly to protect endangered species."

The Forest Resource Education Center (FREC) in Jackson Township is an office of the New Jersey Department of Parks and Forestry.

From the NJDEP website: "The Forest Resource Education Center pine barrens forest provides many recreational opportunities including hiking, fishing, biking, hunting, nature photography, horseback riding and bike trails."

Ocean County Soil Conservation District's (OCSCD) 27th Annual Barnegat Bay Environmental Educators Roundtable

Category: Government (federal and state)
Website: www.soildistrict.org

An official thank-you letter from the 2024 roundtable encapsulates its importance in the program's office's own words:

Dear Educators,

Thank you for attending Ocean County Soil Conservation District's 27th Annual Barnegat Bay Environmental Educators Roundtable, on Wednesday, April 17.

All of us at OCSCD were excited to greet educators who attended in prior years, and equally thrilled to meet so many new teachers this year. We hope you found value in connecting with exhibitors, networking with other teachers, and participating in the field trip and workshops offered by so many talented and knowledgeable presenters.

One of the highlights of the evening was our amazing Keynote Speaker, Ms. Shaina Brenner, 2nd grade teacher at Elms Elementary School, in Jackson. Here is the link to Shaina's Keynote Presentation, created using Canva: https://www.canva.com/design/DAGCWd1Fb_g/_3oPJG6wFMIWxaCUGLttow/view?utm_content=DAGCWd1Fb_g&utm_campaign=designshare&utm_medium=link&utm_source=editor. Embedded within her slide show are several links, including:

- *NJ Energy Data Center: https://njenergydata.rutgers.edu*

- *NJ Climate Change Resource Center: https://njclimateresourcecenter.rutgers.edu*
- *NJ Climate Change Education Hub: https://njclimateeducation.org*
- *Empowered Program (https://www.empoweredschools.org): This is the website for those interested in learning more about the energy conservation program that can be implemented in schools.*
- *Green Career Day Video (https://www.youtube.com/watch?v=KLNIQG5nBYk): This is a highlight video of the Elms Green Career Day, which was an opportunity for our students to learn about environmentally friendly career paths in the fields of renewable energy, environmental protection, recycling, agriculture, forestry, solid waste management and more.*

Ocean and Nature Conservation Society

Category: Nonprofit
Website: Dissolved after more than forty years (approximately 1966–2006)

There were six original formation members, including Elizabeth (Betty) Dorset Newbury Cooper. Mrs. Betty Cooper was the primary co-founder of the society, adding another historical footprint to her lifetime career achievements, including teaching in Whiting, New Jersey. Other effective leaders of ONACS were Mr. A. Morton Cooper and Mrs. Dorothy Long Hale (1924–1990), who both served as president, field trip coordinators, and board members of the organization.

One of the things that made ONACS so effective was Pearl Schwartz and the role in which she served the nonprofit. As one of the last chairpersons, Janet N. Larson, who presided over retiring the banner of ONACS, puts it:

> *Mrs. Pearl Schwartz was the ONACS conservation and legislation chairperson for many years. She studied most proposed environmental legislation, including the State of New Jersey Pinelands Commission formation legislation and subsequently their CCMP, and made recommendations to both the ONACS Board of Directors and the membership about actions to be taken.*

Elizabeth Meirs Morgan was a member for more than twenty-five years. A quote from Elizabeth Meirs Morgan (1913–2004) in a memoriam booklet highlights what one person—or, better yet, a group of concerned persons—can accomplish together:

> *A threesome, Dorothy Hale, Lois Morris, and Elizabeth formed a very effective research team for the Ocean and Nature Conservation Society. Their very thorough investigations in the field often determined action to be taken on a particular issue. The Society was a key force in Ocean County in the creation of the Pinelands Commission. The Nature Center and all of the activities of Cattus Island County Park were developed with the encouragement, planning and support of the Society.*

Pinelands Commission

Category: Government (federal and state)
Website: https://www.nj.gov/pinelands

In 1978, Congress created the first national reserve, the New Jersey Pinelands National Reserve, starting the preservation of the unique ecosystems contained within what ultimately would be a 1.1-million-acre preserve. Unlike national parks, which are mostly conservation areas, the Pinelands is located in parts of seven New Jersey counties, encompassing fifty-six different municipalities. The reserve has active human communities within its borders, and hundreds of thousands of residents and annual visitors freely flow in and out of the Pinelands, which are, in part, governed and/or administered by federal, state and local rule. It was the Pinelands Protection Act of 1979 that established the Pinelands Commission. The New Jersey governor appointed the Pinelands Commission and its members to manage the rules and regulations of the land, their guidance being the Comprehensive Management Plan (CMP) adopted on November 21, 1980. According to NJ.gov, "The New Jersey Pinelands Commission is an independent state agency whose mission is to 'preserve, protect, and enhance the natural and cultural resources of the Pinelands National Reserve, and to encourage compatible economic and other human activities consistent with that purpose.'"

Since the 1960s and up to the formation of the national reserve, the Pinelands region has been threatened with development by what some believed was an obsessive drive to create a jetport in the middle of the Pines. Before John McPhee's book *The Pine Barrens* and before New Jersey Governor Byrne got involved, hundreds of community leaders and environmental groups formed to fight for the environment. Dr. V. Eugene Vivian was among them. Several conferences, the first in 1978, were held with a roster of environmentalists, scientists, ecologists, archaeologists, historians and sociologists in attendance, cosponsored by the Center for Environmental Research, Stockton State College and the Center for Coastal and Environmental Studies at Rutgers University and the New Jersey Department of Environmental Protection. That year, 1978, was a busy one for Doc. Only a handful of noted botanists were on hand (Dr. David Fairbrothers, Dr. Ralph Good, Dr. Silas Little and Dr. Eugene Vivian) for the First Annual Pine Barrens Research Conference, held in Atlantic City in May 1978. On May 22, the Eagle Scout, Dr. Vivian, who had developed his love of flora in Paterson, New Jersey, presented "The Implications of Habitat Researches for Endangered Plant Species of the Pine Barrens," a well-researched paper supporting the argument for the need for disturbance in the Pinelands ecosystems, such as fire.

Pinelands Cultural and Historical Preservation Society (PCS)

Category: Nonprofit
Website: https://www.alberthall.org

One might well wonder why a nonprofit dedicated to preserving the rich musical tradition in the Pines, with the best country and bluegrass bands from the area represented, would be considered a nursery for the environmental education movement in New Jersey. But it's music that moves us to action and helps society pass on knowledge from one generation to the next. On any given Saturday night throughout the year, since 1974, a group of musicians, historians, teachers and environmentalists has gathered down in ol' Waretown, New Jersey, to play music—which continues today. They call these gatherings Sounds of the Jersey Pines. It was preceded by the ol' cabin affectionately known as the Home Place, where bluegrass music gatherings were first held: the Albert Brothers' hunting cabin in Waretown. Who was there in Trenton singing about the preservation of the Pines and what it meant to the local people, the Pineys? None other than the troubadours from Albert Music Hall (125 Wells Mills Road, Route 532, Waretown, New Jersey). PCS just celebrated its fiftieth anniversary at the Hall in Waretown in 2024.

During the same 1978 Pine Barrens Research Conference in Atlantic City where Dr. Vivian spoke, another panelist, Tom Ayres, presented his

Top: Albert Music Hall of Waretown, New Jersey. *Author's collection.*

Bottom: Oak Brand cranberry display hanging on a wall at Albert Music Hall. *Author's collection.*

paper "The Pinelands Cultural Society: Folk Music Performance and the Rhetoric of Regional Pride." A quote from one of the PCS's members in the paper read, "Active organization member Kurt Kiewel says that the music is 'a weapon and a tool for education.'" A noteworthy country singer who sounded like a dead ringer for Patsy Cline played at the Hall and was a charter member of PCS, not to mention a celebrated author of several Pine Barrens folklore books (*Ye Olde Clamtown Almanac*, *The Jersey Devil's Favorite Cranberry Recipes and Folklore* and *The Jersey Devil's Favorite Blueberry Recipes and More Tall Tales*) was Lee M. Gant Thorn. Like Norma Vivian, she had her start in a Pine Barrens community paper and educated the masses in a different way than a traditional teacher in a classroom. News media, popular songs sung and printed books helped spread the Environmental Education ethos. At the *Toms River Reporter*, Thorn developed a ten-part series of articles about the Pine Barens, which became a special print-edition booklet called *Those Picturesque Pinelands*. Through song and story, empathy for the environment is fostered.

From PCS's website,

> *Albert Music Hall is run by the Pinelands Cultural & Historical Preservation Society (PCS), an all-volunteer, non-profit historical society dedicated to the preservation of the Pinelands Cultural Heritage. Since 1974, visitors and musicians have gathered at the hall for live Bluegrass, Country, Folk, Americana, Old Timey & Pinelands Music and to jam in the Pickin' Shed every Saturday night.*

Pinelands Preservation Alliance (PPA)

Category: Nonprofit
Website: https://pinelandsalliance.org

PPA has its roots in 1989 at the General Store in Whitesbog Village; subsequently, its first headquarters was located in Suningive there. As the organization grew to more than twenty employees, the headquarters moved to Pemberton and, later, to their current location at the historic Bishop Farmstead in Southampton, New Jersey. Its mission:

> *To preserve the Pine Barrens ecosystem, promote wide public engagement in the preservation and enjoyment of natural resources, and advance acquisition of land and development rights for conservation.... Through the Pinelands*

> *Adventures* and *The Pinelands Is for Everyone* and *Tour de Pines* (three of their outdoor environmental education initiatives), they help people of all ages, backgrounds, and abilities explore nature through health-giving recreation—and so develop a genuine devotion to environmental protection.

These programs follow the tenets taught at the Conservation and Environmental Studies Center (CESC) at Whitesbog and the New Jersey School of Conservation (SOC) in Stokes State Forest. Information for this section was provided by former PPA trustee Janet Newbury Larson (September 17, 2024).

Pinelands Regional High School

Category: Government (federal and state)
Website: https://www.pinelandsregional.org

Pinelands Regional High School was founded in September 1979 in a little South Jersey town called Little Egg Harbor Township.

The beginning of a similar program to Dr. Vivian's at Whitesbog Village was the Pinelands Experience (a three-day, two-night off-site student outdoor education program) at Pinelands Regional High School. The planning group was Ken Osean, Art Gruber, Terry O'Leary and Cathy O'Leary. Terry recalls,

> *Originally, my wife and I started a program called the Pinelands Experience for all the incoming seventh graders. They'd spend three days out in the woods to bond with other students who didn't know each other from four school districts. A way of bonding is getting them into the environmental theme, and we started that, and when we left, George Young, stepson of Doctor Vivian, took over.*
>
> *In 1979, I was recruited to teach there. I was in Dr. Vivian's environmental science graduate school at Glassboro (now Rowan University). A friend of mine who was in that class too, Tom McCormick, became the chair of the Science Department there at Pinelands Regional High School, and he recruited me. He said, "Look, we're going to do this Pinelands Experience I know what you do at Whitesbog and we'd like to do something similar. And we made no money there, as it was funded by grants. And besides teaching, we had to do research projects on the side. That was our way of making a living. When I got the offer from Pinelands, I reluctantly left*

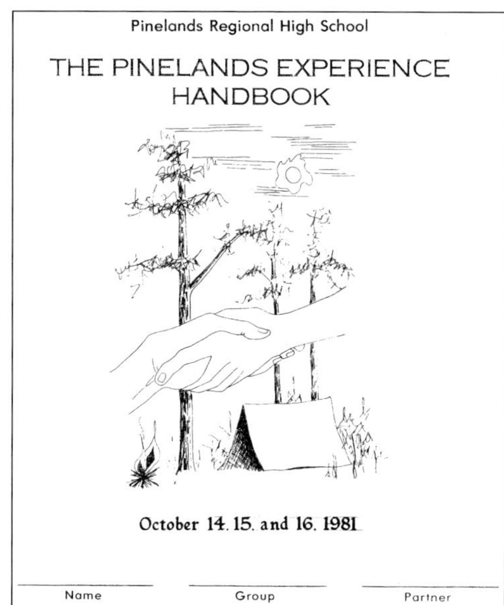

Pinelands Regional High School

THE PINELANDS EXPERIENCE HANDBOOK

October 14, 15, and 16, 1981

Name Group Partner

TABLE OF CONTENTS

Above: Pinelands Experience Handbook from Pinelands Regional High School, October 1981. *Courtesy the O'Leary family.*

Opposite: George Young teaching during Pinelands Experience at Pinelands Regional High School. *Courtesy George and Nadine Young.*

> *Whitesbog. I still lived there. I still taught classes at night at Mount Misery or whatever, to keep the house. After three years, I left Pinelands High School for Ringwood Audubon Weis Ecology Center. Tom McCormick wanted to know what he was going to do. I said, "George is teaching in Haddonfield; maybe he would like to do it." And so it happened: he stepped right in, taking my place.*

In personal correspondence, Christine Raabe of the Ocean County Soil Conservation District suggested another tie Doc Vivian had with Pinelands Regional High School (PRHS), which still exists today through another great teacher's efforts.

> *Jersey-Friendly Yards is currently engaged with the Ocean County Soil Conservation District and one of our flagship programs is Jersey Friendly School Certification (along with the Barnegat Bay Partnership). The PRHS is fortunate to have access to the property behind it, part of the Shourd's Mill Branch watershed and old cranberry bogs.... The project*

85

CENTRAL JERSEY

currently underway is creating an outdoor classroom/trail in the bogs. James Ardoin (Jim) is very *involved in environmental education and has a long history there and is also connected to Terry O'Leary.*

Pinelands Short Course

Organized by Pinelands Commission at Stockton University
Category: Institution of higher education
Website: www.stockton.edu/continuingstudies

Short Course has been held at Stockton since March 2014. Prior, in 2013, it was held at Burlington County College. It first started in 1989 at Rutgers University's Cook College—thirty-five years and going strong.

> *The Pinelands Short Course is open to the public and includes a variety of sessions on topics such as wildlife, plants, land-use/recreation and history and culture. Non-profit organizations and other groups may distribute information and sell Pinelands-themed books and artwork in an exhibition gallery. New Jersey educators who attend can earn professional development credits through the state Department of Education.*

Save Barnegat Bay

Category: Nonprofit
Website: https://savebarnegatbay.org

Founded in 1971, Save Barnegat Bay is another South Jersey entity with a big component of public awareness and education.

> *Our vision is a healthy, vibrant Barnegat Bay ecosystem preserved and protected by active and engaged decision-makers and communities.*
>
> *Our mission is to help restore and protect Barnegat Bay by collaborating with and empowering individuals and communities to live in harmony with our precious watershed. We advance our mission by being a strong and independent voice for the Bay in both waterfront and inland (upstream) communities, as well as at the state level.*
>
> *Our identity: Save Barnegat Bay (SBB) acts as both a leader and facilitator in defending Barnegat Bay's natural environment through education, outreach, and advocacy, with community roots anchored in our*

EcoCenter Headquarters in Toms River, New Jersey. We are proactive as we build upon our strong connection to the Bay, our science-driven environmental expertise, our collaboration with other organizations, and our credibility as a 50-plus-year-old community-based nonprofit with a record of impact and accomplishment.

Our volunteers, staff and donors generously support the work of SBB, giving us flexibility and a strong foundation from which we grow.

We have four core functions:

- *Education and outreach*
- *Grassroots mobilization against threats*
- *Legal and policy action*
- *Collaboration with other watersheds for state-wide action*

Weis Ecology Center (became the New Weis Center for Education, Arts & Recreation)

Category: Nonprofit
Website: http://www.highlandsnaturefriends.orghistory.html

In the mid-1990s, the New Jersey Audubon Society took ownership of the Weis Ecology Center, and in November 2015, this place of historical significance and natural beauty was taken over by the 501(c)(3) organization known as the Highlands Nature Friends Inc. From its website:

> *We are now the proud owners of 152 acres of this beautiful piece of the Highlands, with its rich history and great potential. We have an expanded mission to make the center a vibrant cultural, historical, and natural resource for the community. To reflect that vision, and to honor the family that endowed the center, we chose to rename it "The New Weis Center for Education, Arts & Recreation."*

Terry O'Leary, a foil for much of the teaching his mentor Dr. Vivian (from 1976 to 2008) had imparted to him over many years, also had a short stint with the Weis Ecology Center, promoting environmental education there:

> *When I was offered the job at Pinelands Regional High School, I reluctantly left Whitesbog. I still lived there, so I had to go at night to teach classes at Mount Misery. After three years at Pinelands, I was offered a job at the Weis Ecology Center in Ringwood, New Jersey. The house came with*

a beautiful log cabin in the woods, so I moved from Whitesbog to teach environmental education. Both Cathy and I left to work at Weis, and we were only there for about a year. After that, we started our own landscaping business. I also worked with Doc in his consulting business, ACES.

Whitesbog Preservation Trust

Category: Nonprofit
Website: https://whitesbog.org

From the Whitesbog.org website,

The Whitesbog Preservation Trust invites visitors to travel back in time to learn about the history of cranberry farming, life in a rural South Jersey company town and the individuals and culture that supported the farming operations and Elizabeth White's efforts to cultivate the first highbush blueberry. Explore the village on your own, attend a scheduled program, or sign up for a guided tour. Check our Calendar of Events for dates and times. Registering is easy and can be done online.

Opposite: The active arts and cultural aspect of the village of Whitesbog is promoted at the Whitesbog Art Gallery. *Author's collection.*

Left: Sign on-site at the Barrel Factory in Whitesbog Village. *Author's collection.*

Below. Event hosted at Suningive by Whitesbog Preservation Trust, October 12, 2019. *Author's collection.*

Clockwise from top, left: Holiday wreath workshop, December 1, 2019. Mother Rachel Penrose and her son Lucas enjoy family time; Holiday wreath workshop, December 1, 2019. Colin and his wife, Megan Hilburn and children making family memories at Whitesbog Village wreath workshop; Holiday wreath workshop, December 1, 2019. There's always something fun to do and learn at the wreath workshop and other events hosted by Whitesbog Preservation Trust year-round; Holiday wreath workshop, December 1, 2019. Mother and son making memories at the wreath workshop hosted by Whitesbog Preservation Trust. *Author's collection.*

The trust is a 501(c)(3) nonprofit that is the caretaker of the current Whitesbog Village, established in 1984, which hosts an annual blueberry festival, local artist gatherings at the Whitesbog Art Gallery and so much more.

Pinelands Institute for Natural and Environmental Studies (PINES)

As the CESC sunsetted in 1983–84, Glassboro State professor Gary Patterson, successor to Dr. Vivian, established a new environmental studies program named PINES (Pinelands Institute for Natural and Environmental Studies). Paraphrasing from a survey titled Whitesbog Village and Cranberry Bog HALS No. NJ-1, "In the beginning, the entity was located in the General Store, providing hands-on science programs for school groups about the Pine Barrens ecosystem and other topics." PINES is currently supported by the nonprofit Whitesbog Preservation Trust, formed in 1982 when the original lease agreement between the trust and the New Jersey Department of Environmental Protection (NJDEP) was signed.

Chapter 10

INSPIRED YET?

Whales eat krill, Fish eat krill. Penguins eat fish that eat krill. Seals eat fish and penguins that eat krill. If the krill population crashes, the structure of the food web suggests that all species "above" krill will crash too. In this fragile food web, krill are considered a keystone species because of their essential role in holding together the ecological community.

—Charles Saylan and Daniel T. Blumstein, The Failure of Environmental Education (And How We Can Fix It), *2011*

Oak Sapling Testimonials

One common theme among those lifelong educators who knew Doc Vivian or are still in the field of environmental education found that the job was hard, so very hard, yet so worth it! The job of being a teacher is difficult, especially as humankind's technology becomes more pervasive in and out of the classroom. Give a teacher a curriculum and a pupil, and class can begin. Oh, if it were only so easy. Another commonality that emerged, as you may have already guessed, having read this far, is that yes, nature is a web, but so is the network of torchbearers for education and especially for EE. As the Olympic torchbearer symbolizes the start of something big and the passing of knowledge and experiences to the next generation, so too are our humble oak saplings who have grown to be mighty oaks interrelated and interconnected. Many are of the opinion, and rightly so, that teachers are somewhat of a keystone species. Saylan and Blumstein write that keystone species' essential role is to hold the community together, and where would we be without the glue of our teaching community?

> *The ultimate goal of Environmental Education is to create a citizenry that is environmentally literate. Laypersons must be able to marshal facts to support decisions about projected environmental changes and developments and also must have the commitment to engage in appropriate societal action to implement the desired changes.*
>
> —*Dr. V. Eugene Vivian,*
> Sourcebook for Environmental Education, *1973*

The goal of environmental education, creating environmentally literate citizens, exists today—even after so many mighty oaks like Rachel Carson, Dr. Vivian or Dr. Rillo, who taught for countless years, have passed from this Earth. No applause is ever expected for past accomplishments of the torchbearers of EE, and life on Earth continues to burn. Being dedicated to your work in a sometimes thankless society is worthy of a round of applause, applause for those who bore the burden for so many years and still found time to drop acorns on the ground, planting the oak trees of tomorrow. Teachers, rejoice! Not a teacher? It doesn't matter. If you're an earthling, you call this planet home, and we only have one! Small enclaves of normal people fight for preservation and good stewardship in hopes of fostering a better tomorrow for us and Mother Earth. Finally, you are not alone. Remember: it takes a village. For now, listen and be inspired by the many voices who, maybe, just like you, strive to keep the fire burning!

Friends, Educators, New Jerseyans, Acorns and Mighty Oaks

> *I didn't have a job, so I started off doing some maintenance work. Everything that went on in Whitesbog at that time was the result of Dr. Vivian receiving a Title III federal grant to develop an environmental education center. At one time, there were twenty or thirty workers and staff members working at Whitesbog. Students from all over the state would come to Whitesbog and do environmental education lessons and learn about the Pinelands.*

In some cases, we would get to the school to teach them about Whitesbog. Everything at that point centered around environmental education and Whitesbog in particular, and the Pinelands as well. The Conservation and Environmental Studies Center (CESC) was the environmental education center, through a Title III federal grant, run by Dr. Vivian. (In September 1966, USOE approved the planning grant for $39,000 under Title III of the Elementary and Secondary Education Act.)

Dr. Vivian received a twenty-five-year lease for a dollar a year to do that. The CESC at Whitesbog Village became one of the largest in the country at the time. Schools came from all over the state to learn about Whitesbog. We taught a series of thirty or forty different hands-on direct experience lessons. The students would do activities in the classroom before they came there. They came to Whitesbog and did the hands-on direct experiences, and we'd leave them with follow-up activities. We would call them Day Lessons. "Come out and learn about the Pinelands in a day." Or we would give them unit plans as well.

I was in Vietnam for two years. When I came back, people hated me. I couldn't get a job. I came here and had never heard of the Pinelands and couldn't tell you where it was on a map. I moved into Whitesbog and started as a maintenance worker, and gradually, I would go out with some of the other teachers while they were doing the lessons. When I saw them do that, it sparked an interest in my life that I devoted the next fifty years to: studying and learning about the Pinelands and trying to pass that on to other people. It changed my life. And because it changed my life, it changed a lot of other people's lives that I influenced over the past fifty or sixty years.

Dr. Vivian was by far the smartest person I ever met. And I'm not just saying that because I'm his stepson. When I got inducted into the Pine Barrens Hall of Fame as an Honoree in Education, there were three of us that went through a program where we were taught all that we knew by my dad, Dr. Eugene Vivian, but he wasn't inducted. I couldn't believe it. He has done and learned and taught more about the Pinelands than I know. He loved it. His whole life was dedicated to teaching people about it. His influence on so many people throughout his career has been amazing. He was someone who loved the Pine Barrens with all his heart and instilled that love in others. And with that love of the Pine Barrens to protect it. There could be a couple of books written about him. The man was amazing. He was National Conservation Educator of the Year; he wrote numerous books himself....You talk to any of the other folks we mentioned. We used to call him Doc. One of them calls me every once in

Family photo taken on March 7, 2024, at Rebecca's Cupboard, Whiting, New Jersey. *Left to right*: Alfred Covell, Rebecca Hopkins, TammySue Marks Hopkins and George Young. *Courtesy Hopkins family.*

a while, and they'll say, "Boy, your dad, I sure miss him. He taught me everything I know." Whitesbog wouldn't be where it is today if it wasn't for him; that isn't an exaggeration.

To me, Whitesbog has been responsible for probably thousands of people interested in the Pinelands and environmental education, and Whitesbog in particular. I used to compare my father, stepfather, Dr. Vivian, to a giant oak tree and that giant oak tree dropped many acorns down on the ground. And they turned into giant oak trees as well. That one person has influenced me, Terry O'Leary, John Szczepanski, George Henkel and on and on. All became environmental leaders in the Pinelands. Terry O'Leary, Christine Raabe and I were inducted into the Pine Barrens Hall of Fame as Honorees in Education together.

—George Young, age seventy-six, stepson of Dr. Eugene Vivian and retired teacher, personal communication, January 8, 2024

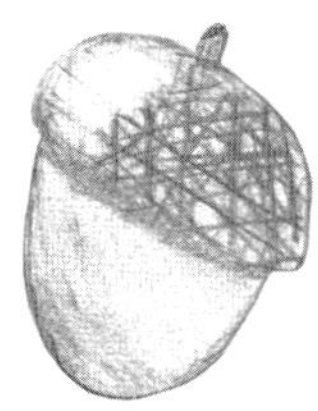

I first met Dr. Vivian through Terry O'Leary and Shaun O'Rourke, who had been a professor of theirs through Glassboro. First time meeting Doc probably around 1980 or and had heard about him being a legend in Environmental Education and environmental science studies. His prodigies, like Terry O'Leary and George Young, were with Pinelands Regional High School. Shaun O'Rourke worked for Ocean County Parks. His protégées were all over the place. For years and years, I worked with Pinelands Regional High School with their environmental program with the county parks to supplement the things they couldn't do. Those guys were there, and we worked together for a long time. George, his stepson of Doc and Terry and Shaun were his students at one time or another.

In South Jersey, he was the legend. I met him through those guys, and we put him on the Cattus Island Advisory Council early on for Cattus Island County Parks. We named the library at the Cooper Environmental Center at Cattus Island after Dr. Vivian. It was because of his help to establish the park here, his advice, and help in a lot of different ways. But that wasn't the only way I knew him.

When they were young: Mike Magnum, Shaun O'Rourke and Dean Chlebowski. *Courtesy Ocean County Parks and Recreation.*

We lived in Little Egg Harbor Township in the 1990s. On opposite sides of town, but I guess we were neighbors. He helped the town establish an environmental commission. It was through his efforts that the township of Little Egg Harbor established an environmental commission, and he was the first chair there. He was there for at least ten years. One day, I got a call from him, and he asked me to join the environmental commission. He had a way of talking; I told him I was pretty busy, but he told me, "Why don't you join the commission with me?" The next year, he retires, and he tells them to appoint me chairman. I think he had this planned all along. He got me on the commission because he wanted to retire from the commission, so he gave me one year on the commission with him, then I became the chairman of Little Egg Harbor because of him. He was a pioneer in many ways, and that was just one.

He had a way of talking. It's hard to describe his way of talking. You listened to what he said because he was always giving you some bit of knowledge that you might not have known, or he gave you a different perspective on something, too. A very hard worker. He was a dedicated and extremely hard worker all the time until he got old and couldn't do things. He lived a long life and was doing things up until his eighties. A lot of older people in the environmental community I've run into over the years had him as a professor. The younger people don't know who I'm talking about. He was a legend, literally.

—Michael Magnum, retired (after forty-six years) director,
Ocean County Department of Parks and Recreation, age seventy,
personal communication, March 22, 2024

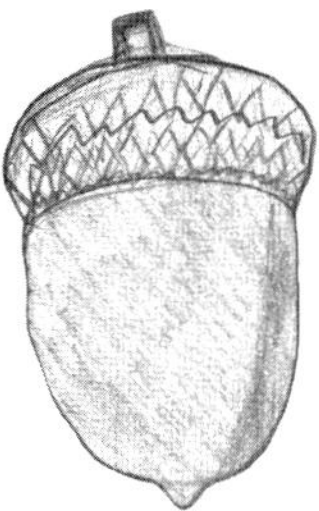

In 2005, I was volunteering and involved in different things. I met Terry O'Leary at the Forest Resource Education Center (FREC), and we talked about the difference in passions if you learn from a book or if you learn because you're doing it. Because you're getting wet, you're getting dirty

Right: Terry O'Leary demonstrating absorption qualities of sphagnum moss at Forest Resource Education Center (FREC) Jackson Township, New Jersey. *Courtesy O'Leary family*.

Below: One of the many nature interpretive stations at the Lighthouse Camp in Waretown, New Jersey. *Courtesy O'Leary family*.

and you're seeing all these different things. In October 2006, I became the caretaker at the Lighthouse Center (Natural Resource Education Foundation) in Waretown until April 2024.

My favorite story is where I'm doing a program basically about wildlife and identifying wildlife from scat found on the ground. Some of the kids in the program had a hard time concentrating. This one young man seemed to not be paying attention. A teacher chaperone said, "Listen, you need to pay attention and come over here." The boy then literally repeated everything I had said, even though he wasn't looking and being engaged because he was in his own space. I try to say to people that everybody learns differently. Some people learn visually, some have to write it down and some have to touch it. But this was an opportunity to let people learn at their own pace. There were times when kids would come in and you were talking about the construct of the book and the lesson plan—they didn't care. But bring out an owl pellet and explain where that owl pellet came from, and now we are going to open it up and see what's inside. They're right there with you.

At the center, there were all these different components like birding, wildlife and pioneer homesteading. We had kids who would come from the city who never had walked on a dirt road before. Or who had never seen a horseshoe crab, and it was frightening to see something that kind of looked like a dinosaur, something that came out of the past. To be able to watch them go from, "I don't want to be here!" to "Wow, that's a fiddler crab, look at that thing go!" What a change.

—Pola Girard Galie, volunteer naturalist, age seventy-one,
personal communication, April 3, 2024

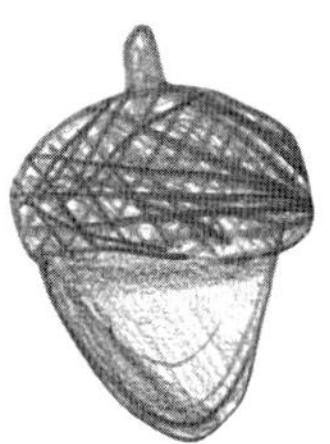

I knew Doc from 1972 to 2002. I wasn't a peer; he was No. 1. I was a competitor, but neither of us ever found any competition between each other. He knew things had a lifespan and it ran its lifespan. I tell people that if you don't keep the culture up, when it gets broken, it's very difficult to bring it

back. You have to reinvent the wheel. An awful lot of people that work in the county parks are someone who had worked for me beforehand. The newbies caught up with the culture. They could make their own decisions on how to do things, but they knew how things could run before they set out on their own. The only way you live forever is to teach a culture to keep the culture going. And that's what Doc Vivian did, too. He was the predecessor to that.

At the CESC, they did not have a facility museum. They were mostly an "outside doing things" program. Not just talking about the environment but moving things like mathematics and English literature outside, trying to get the environmental stuff incorporated in the general curriculum so that you couldn't tell that you were talking about the environment even though you were. But Doc was a naturalist and a teacher. When you can cross that line and be both, that's the thing. Part of the problem with the environmental movement today: it got incorporated. It's almost like people take it for granted. An awful lot of the environmental ed had to fit into the core curriculum to get it into the classrooms and have it included in the curriculum. So that was all part of the gain. And Doc was always trying to get that blend done. Those bunch of people who were working at Whitesbog became elementary teachers.

One of the reasons I went to Glassboro State College as a college student was to take a course with Dr. Vivian. I never got to take a class with him as it seemed he was always on sabbatical when I tried, but he was my advisor for a couple of grants I received down there. He gave me very helpful advice and grants on floodplains and wetlands. I was setting up an environmental center at Rough Acres Campground at the time for colleges and college students. His information and stuff made that center work better. Doc gave me the curriculum used at the CESC. He never said no. After he retired and moved to Tuckerton, he was on my advisory council at Cattus Island. He was very beneficial there to keep things on the straight and narrow, and he was very influential in getting a couple of people hired down there. One of them set up another environmental center down in Waretown at Wells Mills Park, a German Georgieff.

Frankly, there was no one else in the advisory council who could come close to his credentials. His influence was significant when it came to hiring and firing and staffing programs that we were doing. In the actual park itself, the environmental area, he was helpful with mapping out and identifying the wetlands and the various habitats there, and as an advisory council per se, he helped get the county to go along with the idea of building a deck out in front of the environmental center for viewing through a large donation. The main thing was, he was the expert. He was the environmental science expert, the environmental educator expert that you could rely on for information. I was the chief naturalist and ran the place. Back then, Doc was one of the "earls", what would you say in Jersey—he was one of the first-generation environmental people.

Doc did a lot of Lancasterian system–based teaching in the one-room schoolhouse. He taught the teachers to teach the students to teach the students. The teacher would teach the older kids something, and they would teach the younger kids. Then the younger kids would teach the younger students. It incorporated the people who were involved in the learning of the stuff, and it made things work because you kept reinforcing their learning by doing. The old one room schoolhouse…Doc had no ego; he was laid-back. So laid-back that when he would give a talk, he was quiet. I had, one night, an advisory council meeting, and he called up to say he wasn't coming to the meeting. He was at the hospital and had to have his stomach pumped because he ate the wrong mushroom. He never gave up.

When he closed down CESC at Whitesbog, he donated all the books and curriculum stuff to Cattus. He had built an expansive set of nature studies, nature lesson plans and activities and programs along with books. They named the library at Cattus Island after him. [Similarly, the SOC library is named after Dr. Vivian's counterpart Dr. L.B. Sharp.] *If you wanted to do something, Doc had already done it and had a curriculum developed for it. When Doc got involved in Whitesbog, he hired a bunch of students from Glassboro and other places and put them to work. Unfortunately, when he got ready to retire, no one was there to pick up the ball. They were all off on their adventures. Terry O'Leary was up in North Jersey running Weis Environmental Center. A couple of them, like George Young, were teachers and didn't want to leave their good jobs, and things just fell to the wayside when Doc retired.*

—Shaun O'Rourke, a sunbird from Florida to New Jersey, once chief naturalist of Ocean County Cattus Island Park, age seventy, personal communication, May 31, 2024

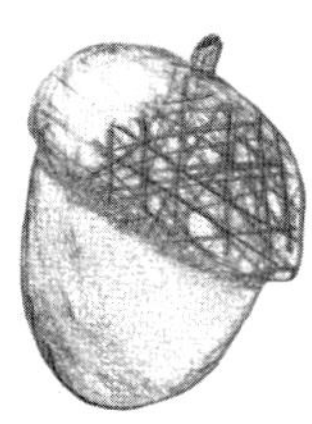

I taught [twenty-seven years to date] *next to George Young at Pinelands Regional High School. George and I taught next to each other for years. I met Dr. Vivian on many different occasions. I didn't learn from him, I didn't take any classes with him through Rowan, but I did know him through George. As I'm working my way around folks. there's a net. There's this web of people who studied with Dr. Vivian who went on and had their own careers. Another teacher, Joe Palumbo, worked with Dr. Vivian on the surveys. The world is so small, and the web is so large, once you start to find out who's who. A woman who taught with my dad, Sam Ardoin, a seventh-grade math teacher at Pemberton, was another in that web. Dr. Patti Duncan, who grew up in Browns Mills, took all those courses at Rowan with Doc.*

A whole bunch of them didn't just stick around in the Pine Barrens. They—Gary, Joe Palumbo, George Young and Dr. Vivian—traveled to Canada and other places to study ecosystems.

Research trips and such. [In plant geography class during the summer, students were required to trace two, three and sometimes up to five Pinelands plants and track each plant's distribution along the coast to its northern reaches, sometimes in Nova Scotia (for example, *Lophiola aurea*, or goldencrest), and a plant's southern limits along the coastal Atlantic plain (for example, *Gentiana autumnalis*, pine barren gentian).] *In June 2023, George Young came up from Tennessee and talked with my class at Pinelands. I was in Denver recently for the National Science Teacher Association Conference. At my supervisor's suggestion, I put up a proposal to talk about what we were doing at Pinelands. We were offered an hour-long presentation. I spoke about the Barrens to Bay class. Not so much about the class and the curriculum or what to do when you have forty-five acres, because not everybody has abandoned cranberry bogs like we have. Just get your kids outside anywhere to do some science, but more importantly, get the people in the surrounding area who are experts in the field. There are all these places trying to do educational outreach. They understand you can't do field trips like we used to do as kids. So they're willing to come to you because their organization (nonprofits and state groups), when it received certain federal funding, it's a requirement, education and outreach. Call them to ask them to talk to your class about*

Opposite and following page: Dr. Vivian on a Florida vacation/botany trip. *Courtesy O'Leary family.*

what kind of projects they are doing. When you have all these people in the community, it takes a village.

Let's get these kids out there and expose them to career paths. Major paths, where to study, how to study, who to study with—and let's give them perspective on what they can do. Groups like Ocean County Soil Conservation District, under the leadership of its director Christine Raabe,

Above: Pine barren gentian, *Gentiana autumnalis. Author's collection.*

Left: Goldencrest, *Lophiola aurea. Author's collection.*

are a great example. We've been involved in three grants with them; Jersey-Friendly Yards certified, southern Barnegat Bay watershed grants and we're part of Stockton's red maple grant this year.

—James Ardoin, teacher of Barrens to Bay Ecology and Anatomy and Physiology at Pinelands Regional High School, age forty-nine, personal communication, April 15, 2024

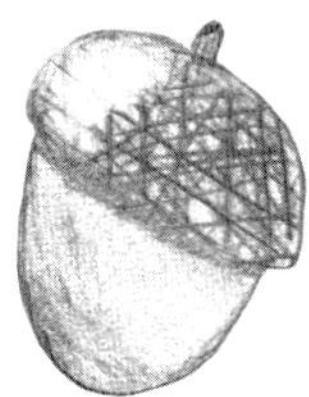

Here is a favorite quote of mine, "Never doubt that a small group of thoughtful, committed citizens can change the world. Indeed, it is the only thing that ever has." One of the points I wanted to make about "hope for the future" stems directly from my experience with the annual Barnegat Bay Environmental Educators Roundtable [which celebrated its twenty-seventh year in 2024] *Each year, I ask for a show of hands of how many teachers have attended: every year, fifteen years or more, ten years, five years, first time, etc. Some people still attend that have for the entire twenty-seven—although some have passed or retired (obviously)—but there is still—and it seems to be an increasing percentage of "first timers." There is a whole new group of educators carrying forward EE. This might provide some inspiration for how your book may end—by not ending at all—as the next generation of educators is present, engaged and actively seeking how to make their lessons relative.*

I was born to be a teacher. My father was a mighty oak from Cook College of Rutgers University, a teacher of teachers. I grew up in East Brunswick, where you could go to Rutgers, or you could go to Rutgers or you could choose Rutgers. I went to Rutgers as an undergraduate and entered into environmental science with a secondary in teaching K–12 certification of science. I met Dr. Vivian. I'm not a mighty oak; I'm a sapling. Terry O'Leary is one of my mentors. I graduated from Cook College in 1985. I'm a little bit younger than some of the other folks, but I feel like they are all my mentors: Terry O'Leary, Dr. Vivian, Elizabeth Morgan, who I nicknamed Mother Nature of Ocean County.

Dr. Vivian was up in age then, and you could tell he had a world of experience. He had already planted acorns all over the place. He had a wealth of information, and he had a sense of humor. He sort of lived the awareness to action: a true environmentalist. He kind of launched me into environmental work in Ocean County. "I have a perfect job for you. It doesn't pay, but it's a great job for you: Cattus Island Advisory Council. You're young; you've got enthusiasm; you'd be a great member of the advisory council." Which at that point in his career he was trying to wind down and find replacements for positions he once held. I was inducted into the advisory council, and slowly, Dr. Vivian backed away. Awareness to action: ultimately, the action is the stewardship, is where you want to get the ultimate goal. Making people aware of environmental issues and concerns is the first step. Getting the awareness, the skills and knowledge and having them do something about it: that's the ultimate action part.

If you went through Barnegat Bay Steward, you're a steward. Here's where you want everyone to get. They don't have to save the world; they have to save one oak tree at a time. You can't do this all in a classroom. The outdoors has to be the classroom. That's also the lesson of environmental education. You can make your students aware of the environment, but immersing yourself in it makes it or helps lead to that stewardship. The outdoor movement in the '60s, '70s, and '80s was really about how to create a responsible ethical citizen of the planet. If people don't experience it, it's not real to them. If you don't know about it, how are you going to care about it? Our culture is not as connected with the natural world as it has evolved to be.

—Christine Raabe, district director at Ocean County Soil Conservation District, age sixty, personal communication, February 29, 2024

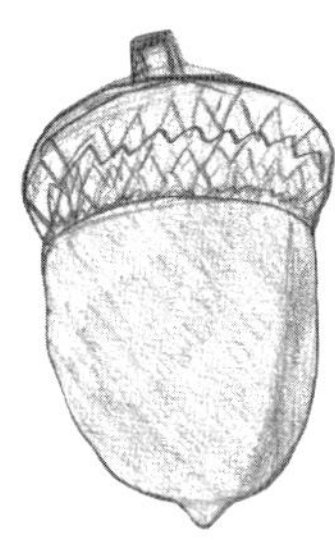

One of the biggest things I got from Dr. Vivian—it's related to his teaching method—was a question that he would often tell you to use. A single one-word question: "Why?" So when we were out there in the field, and you noticed something—and some of the people I work with got to the point where they noticed these things, too. For instance: the forest is just a little bit different. Like when you're driving down the dirt road from Harrisville to Martha. You're getting closer to Martha, and the forest changes. It's hard to describe or put your finger on it, but you can see the difference. When you encounter something like that you ask, "Why?"

I'm driving down the road, and suddenly there's a bunch of black walnuts or Norway spruces: "Why?" Without thinking twice: "Something happened here; there must have been a homestead, part of a farm." Here at Wells Mills Park, when I take students on a nature walk and we take the trail that leaves the nature center down the slope towards the lake, suddenly you come to big holes in the ground, big pits. I'll ask the kids what looks different here, what looks unnatural. Some of them will spot, and some won't. And I'll ask, "Why, what do you think happened?" In this instance, they were mining clay, which was to be shipped to Trenton via railroad.

German Georgieff in the classroom representing Ocean County Parks and Recreation. *Courtesy Ocean County Parks and Recreation.*

German Georgieff in an outdoor classroom representing Ocean County Parks and Recreation. *Courtesy Ocean County Parks and Recreation.*

But no matter what you encounter—it could be the behavior of a bird or whatever—the first thing that should come to mind is, "Why?" Whether you can figure it out yourself or look for the answers from books and other people. But that was one of the biggest Dr. Vivian would talk about. You didn't have to know what you were looking at. But you had to ask the question why it was there and why it was happening. And that would lead you to more knowledge. And he was big on that one thing, Dr. Vivian.

It all doesn't start as an organized effort. It starts with separate individual efforts that end up cooperating and forming connections. Eventually, you have something more organized, like the Pinelands National Reserve or the CESC Inc. that Dr. Vivian created at Whitesbog Village. Things grow out of smaller individual efforts. I know many people who would say that if there was an environmental hall of fame, Dr. Vivian would be nominated as one of the key members. Terry O'Leary and the late Howard Boyd would say that. When Boyd was writing his first field guide to the Pine Barrens, he requested Dr. Vivian to cowrite the book with him. Instead, Doc volunteered to write the foreword. They were of the same generation, but I know he had the highest respect for Gene. As far as younger people looking up, hero-wise, Joe Arsenault is an environmental consultant. A bit younger than Gene, he taught a wetlands plant ID course for Rutgers University with Ted Gordon. That web is one of the more satisfying things of my career. I've gotten to work with or just gotten to know wonderful people who have done wonderful things for history, for the environment. It's probably one of my most valuable things or accomplishments in my career getting to know these people.

—German Georgieff, current Ocean County chief park naturalist, age sixty-three, personal communication, January 26, 2024

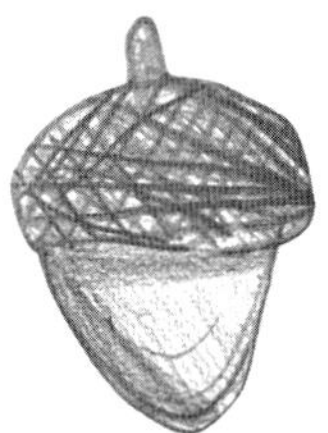

Doc was an inspiration to me. I was a dual major at Rutgers. I got a bachelor's degree in English literature, and I minored in science. When I decided to get into teaching, I wanted to go the environmental science route, so I went back to Glassboro. I loaded up on science and education courses, which is where I hooked up with Doc. He came out of retirement. He started the program in environmental education at Glassboro when I was there. Gary Patterson had taken over the rains there. But Doc came back to teach some of the courses, and that's when I met him, and he introduced me to George Young, and the rest is history.

A lot of the people I met after at Pinelands or different places were somehow connected to Doc. I spent a lot of time out in the field with Doc. We'd go out together, and he just blew me away. He was amazing. He ran a class up at Montclair State College, up along the Delaware Water Gap. Montclair had a facility up there, and about a dozen of us in the class went. We stayed in rudimentary dorms. We ended up walking up the mountain there, and the class was about the changes in vegetation at different elevations. Doc knew I was a birder. We'd be hiking along, and he'd point out different trees, flowers and shrubs, calling out their names in Latin. He knew everything; he knew every tree and every bush. So I thought to myself, I'm going to impress him. This was in the spring. A bird would start singing, and I would call it out. He'd look at me and say, "Very good." Then another bird would call out, and I'd call it out. Finally, the third bird called out, and he called it out. I looked at him and said, "Man, is there anything that you don't know?" He was the last of the true Renaissance men. He knew Greek and Latin, and he knew everything. He was an amazing, amazing man. And to make it even more amazing, he was in his seventies then, and we were hiking up fairly steep terrain. He was leading the class up those hills. An amazing guy, he really was. I still think about him to this day and smile every time I think about it.

At night, we went to the local bar. "Let's knock off and get a beer and everybody relax." I think Doc is probably going to bed by eight o'clock. By ten or eleven o'clock we were all like, "Doc, we got to get some sleep." He was still telling stories. He was an amazing guy. Gives me a big grin just thinking about it.

—Joe Palumbo, retired teacher, age seventy-seven,
personal communication, January 29, 2024

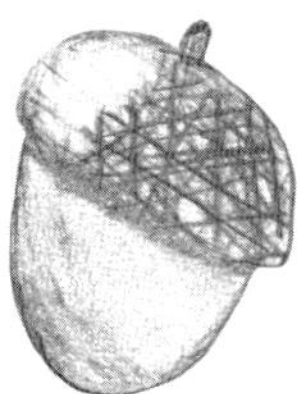

I was kindred sisters with Cathy O'Leary when we worked at Wells Mills County Park. You want to teach the kids; you want to take them out to show them things, to teach them outside. I'm not educated in the environmental numbers or the facts of things out there. I'm just a wild barefoot child who grew up in the woods and just loves it. I know my plants, know my birds—not all. I know a little about everything but not a lot about it all. Mike Magnum taught me everything I knew about the woods.

I was a teacher's aide at one point. We were canoeing as guests with Ocean County Parks and Recreation. And I asked the guide, "How did they get this job?" He said, "I applied." So I applied, and Mike interviewed me, and I was hired. I could have been dropped off in the middle of the

Above: Cathy O'Leary and Lillian Hoey Gomez at Alloway Farm monument. *Courtesy O'Leary family.*

Left: Grave marker of the legendary Joe Mulliner, a famous Pine Robber. *Courtesy O'Leary family.*

Opposite, top: Lillian Hoey Gomez and Cliff Oakley giving a talk to students at Ocean County Wells Mills Park. *Courtesy O'Leary family.*

Opposite, middle: Sign in the Pines: "Ticknchigger Way." *Courtesy O'Leary family.*

Opposite, bottom: Lillian Hoey Gomez at Brooksbrae Terra Cotta Brick Factory, circa 1990s. *Courtesy O'Leary family.*

LET IT SNOW

TICKNCHIGGER WAY

woods, but I could find my way. And along the way, I'll see turtles or birds or that flower, what tree is that and the sound of the water. If you are born and raised in the woods as a wild child, nobody is going to take it from you.

A teacher I had in 1957 at Southern Regional High School, Tom Regen, said, "OK class, we're going outdoors. OK, stop where you are, get down on the ground and look down at what you see. Now draw it." I was near British soldier lichen, maybe eleven or twelve, and I drew it, and I still remember it today. He was a great teacher, like Terry O'Leary. He and Mike always told me I could do things I thought I couldn't. Proud to be Piney, barefoot and wild.

—Lillian Hoey Gomez, former park naturalist of Ocean County and Lady in White Of Piney Folklore from 1988 to 2002, age seventy-eight, personal communication, March 15, 2024

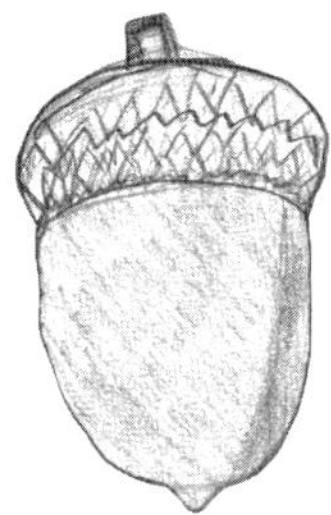

I knew Doc since 1962, but after he retired from Glassboro, I didn't see him as much. He always understated; in other words, he didn't promote himself. He promoted his ideas, promoted and helped people with their careers. Overwhelmingly, the thing he did that was not mainstream in teaching was that he brought the classroom out of doors. So many people taught biology and environmental sciences in the confines of a traditional classroom environment and used slides, photographs and samples in the classroom. Dr. Vivian's approach was: those things that would best be learned in the out-of-doors should be taught out-of-doors, and those things that were best addressed in the classroom should be addressed in the classroom.

So whenever you go to his class, you had better be dressed for going outdoors. Whether it was a lab or not or you had a class after or not, he would take the class out. "We are going to look at this stream. We saw this in the stream the other day and we're all going to go wade over there today." He did such a fantastic job of organizing content and pedagogy. He was just a natural. I don't think we appreciated it at the time. We thought

Dr. Eugene Vivian with youth and a snake. *Courtesy the O'Leary family*.

maybe all college professors were supposed to be that way, but after our four years of school, we learned that that was probably the thing that made him different—and the fact that he taught in an interdisciplinary way. The lines of disciplines weren't sacred to him. He would teach a little bit of history of the Pine Barrens while teaching his biology of the Pine Barrens. He never apologized for that. He felt that was the way you learned things, from integrating information and subject areas.

He would always say, "Teach for the big ideas." Teach for what he called—and what eventually became a mantra in science education—conceptual schemes. Forging the big ideas. Complementary of organisms and the environment. Relationships between species. The evolution of organisms through time. He would teach these big ideas in science, and he would build on them and have students synthesize them. It was a different way of teaching. I had to believe he studied learning theory without ever telling us. He set us up for success. All the people that encountered him, especially the science orientated, were so enthralled by him and how he did.

Doc talked about L.B. Sharp all the time. He invited L.B. Sharp to Glassboro for lunch downtown at a sub shop one time with the class. Between a peer and a mentor, Doc would quote him all the time. There were two forces at the time in education. Professor Dr. Thomas J. Rillo was an outdoor educator who came from the world of outdoor education. There was a difference between outdoor education and environmental education. The outdoor educators were more recreational or camping education and appreciation of the outdoors. And environmental education was more of science and public policy. Dr. Rillo came to Glassboro College as the graduate advisor to the master's program. In that first class, Gary Patterson was with me; Professor Rillo was the graduate advisor.

Doc had a talent for teaching. He'd ask questions like, "Tommy, how do you know that? Tell me about it. How do you know that?" That was his expression. "You said something good and valuable. But I'm really curious about how you learned it and how you came to understand that idea or that concept. Tell me more about it." That is what he was getting at. He was interested in how people learn things and how they acquire knowledge. He was not only an environmentalist but a good educational psychologist. He was way ahead of his time in certain things. Interested in thought processes and how people inquire about information, knowledge and points of view. He didn't believe we should separate science, technology or public policy from things like ethics, morality and values.

—Dr. Thomas Gallia, vice president and professor emeritus, Rowan University (1962–present) age eighty, personal communication, August 13, 2024

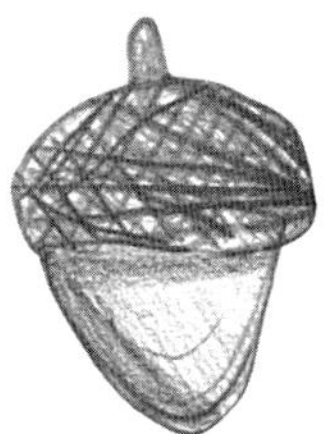

Originally, at Pinelands, my wife [Cathy O'Leary, née Reres] *and I started a program called the Pinelands Experience. All the incoming seventh graders at the Pinelands Regional High School would spend three days out in the woods to bond with other students from four school districts. Those kids didn't know each other. It was a way for them to bond and to get them into the environmental theme. There, at the beginning of 1979, I had been in Dr. Vivian's environmental science graduate school at Glassboro. A friend of mine in my class, Tom McCormick, recruited me, as he was*

JAMES J. FLORIO
1st District, New Jersey

WASHINGTON OFFICE:
1726 Longworth House Office Building
Washington, D.C. 20515
(202) 225-6501

DISTRICT OFFICES:
23 South White Horse Pike
Somerdale, New Jersey 08083
(609) 627-8222

114 East High Street
Glassboro, New Jersey 08028
(609) 881-7050

Congress of the United States
House of Representatives
Washington, D.C. 20515

COMMITTEES:
INTERSTATE AND FOREIGN COMMERCE
HEALTH AND THE ENVIRONMENT SUBCOMMITTEE
TRANSPORTATION AND COMMERCE SUBCOMMITTEE

INTERIOR AND INSULAR AFFAIRS
NATIONAL PARKS AND INSULAR AFFAIRS SUBCOMMITTEE

PERMANENT SELECT COMMITTEE ON AGING
FEDERAL, STATE AND COMMUNITY SERVICES SUBCOMMITTEE
RETIREMENT INCOME AND EMPLOYMENT SUBCOMMITTEE

February 20, 1978

Mr. Terence M. O'Leary, Staff Consultant
Conservation & Environmental Studies Center
Post Office Box 7596, RD 7
Browns Mills, New Jersey 08015

Dear Mr. O'Leary:

The time and energies you provided in helping to make the workshop a success was certainly appreciated. Programs, such as the one offered at the Center, are beneficial in helping our state's educators teach their students about the uniqueness of the Pinelands. And your support of the recent workshop aided in achieving that goal.

Thanking you again for your help, I remain

Sincerely yours,

J J Florio

JAMES J. FLORIO
Member of Congress

JJF/s

PLEASE RESPOND TO
WASHINGTON ( ) SOMERDALE ( ) GLASSBORO ( )

Signed letter from Congressman James J. Florio addressed to Terry O'Leary and the CESC. *Courtesy O'Leary family.*

the chairman of the science department at the high school. He said, "Look, we're going to do this Pinelands experience, and I know what you do at Whitesbog." And we made no money at Whitesbog; we were all funded by grants.

The impact of Doc's work at Whitesbog was tremendous. When they wanted to have and pass Pinelands legislation, we invited Congressman Jim Florio to come to Whitesbog to see us teach a class. He watched us teach kids about Pinelands ecology, and then we got into a Greyhound bus and went through all dirt roads to Sweetwater Casino for a conference. There he signed the legislation, and we thought that was a big deal.

It was ironic because once they started the Pinelands Commission, Dr. Vivian was on the education committee. George Young's wife, Nadine, was the secretary to the director there. Whenever we wanted to represent a client who wanted to develop something in the Pine Barrens, we had to go before the Pinelands Commission. They would send people out to the field to check our work. These were people either Dr. Vivian or I had taught. And now they were regulating us. We'd joke and say to them, "Don't you remember what I taught you?" "This is why this is a wetland; this is why this needs a buffer." I had a lot of people who I taught along the way who are now doing their own thing in their field, whether they're working for the forest fire service, or recycling or ecology, trail system-rail trail, or Ocean County naturalists.

All those things added up, I think. I was sort of spread out too thin, maybe. I was diversified in teaching about it, doing fieldwork for it, and helping movements go along to acquire land or do programs. I wrote a little book in 2000, Ecotour Trail Guide to Great Bay Boulevard. *The best thing is passing it on and sharing it. I always tried to seek out people who could teach you or mentor you. That was a plus, and I tried to pass it on.*

—Terry O'Leary, retired ecologist, age seventy-six, personal communication, January 10, 2024

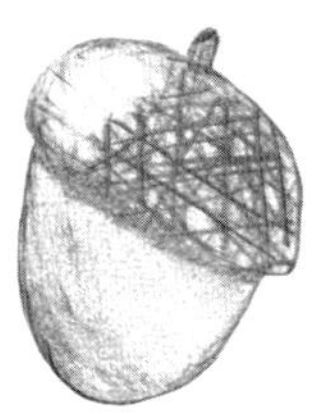

About thirty years ago, I worked at the New Jersey Sea Grant Consortium. A lot was going on in the late '90s in Barnegat Bay. We had just gotten the bay declared a National Estuary Program. Many of us had been involved before that for about a decade putting together a watershed management plan, which allowed us to go to the next step to begin the estuary program. I called up a bunch of colleagues and said, "We're all doing pretty cool stuff. Wouldn't it be great if we had a workshop and spread the word to teachers?" So we came up with a common theme within the Barnegat Bay watershed, thinking perhaps we could foster schools throughout the watershed, have some common messages about the bay and the watershed and the environmental issues we were dealing with.

Our objective was really simple. All of us were involved in some kind of conservation and management mode, and we thought, Let's bring that out to the teachers. *It turned out to be a consensus that we should try. And the rest is history. I'm proud that the Ocean County Soil District, several years later, stepped up and took the lead.*

—John Tiedemann, retired Monmouth University professor (twenty-six years), age seventy, speaking at the 27th Annual Barnegat Bay Environmental Educators Roundtable, April 17, 2024

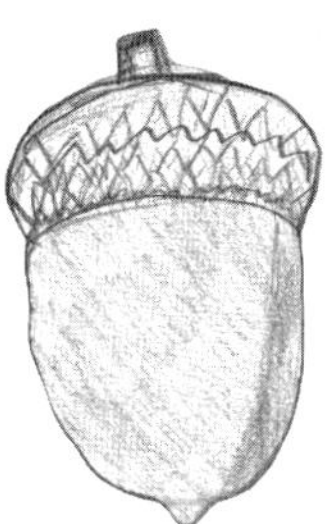

Always the teacher, whether on a hike, van trip, or just a casual walk, Doc would always quiz us on our awareness of the surroundings. For example, he would ask, "What kind of forest are we going through?" One might respond, "Pine/oak forest." Then Doc might grimace! And you would then know to look again, noting that the oak was the dominant species around us, and therefore we were in an oak/pine forest. In this way, Doc demonstrated how things can rapidly change in our environment and the factors that influence change.

Glassboro State College [graduated at Glassboro in 1976] *had what I considered to be an excellent component of their teacher training program. During our junior year, all upcoming teachers were required to take a course that required us to spend a week cabin camping in Stokes State Forest for constant experiential learning. My week at Stokes was the beginning of the second semester. We learned to adapt to our environment with six-plus inches of snow on the ground, and donning snowshoes, we adapted to learning science (including night sky observations), math, literature, etc.*

During my last semester at Glassboro, I became a part-time employee [full-time on graduation] *at Education Improvement Center (EIC) for the State of New Jersey, located in Sewell, New Jersey. I had the good fortune to work for Paul Winkler, as my supervisor, and have Cliff Daniels as a coworker. Our job was to research "hands-on" curriculums that had been developed throughout the country. We would visit various local classrooms to try out many of these lessons and then report back on the feedback from teachers and students. Later, meeting Doc through my husband, Terry, I became further enlightened and practiced improving my own learning and teaching methods. After EIC, I taught for several years at Pinelands Regional, Tuckerton, New Jersey. As one of several coauthors of the "Pinelands Experience," we implemented many of Doc's lessons into the curriculum.*

After a while, we moved to Waretown, New Jersey. I wanted to work at Wells Mills Park, Ocean County, New Jersey. I started as a volunteer and then became a part-time employee, and eventually, a full-time position became available. Mike Mangum was the supervisor. Lillian Hoey Gomez and I ran many park programs together. Lillian is a great storyteller. The best was when she played the Lady in White and Cliff Oakley (1929–2008) played the Jersey Devil. When Cliff retired, I played the Jersey Devil.

After four and a half years with Ocean County Parks, I was offered a sixth-grade science teaching position that I couldn't refuse. I spent sixteen rewarding years at Stafford Intermediate in Manahawkin, New Jersey. With virtual technology now incorporated into learning, I found it increasingly time-consuming as a teacher to incorporate outdoor education and hands-on learning into the current school lessons and curriculum while still meeting local, state and federal mandates. The guidelines are necessary to have students meet certain grade level standards throughout the country. In this way, when families must relocate, students can pick up their learning right where they left off.

Left: Cliff Oakley in a Jersey Devil costume for Ocean County Parks. *Courtesy O'Leary family.*

Below: Cathy O'Leary in the classroom at Stafford Intermediate, Manahawkin, New Jersey. *Courtesy O'Leary family.*

My many accumulated resources from past lessons learned at Stokes, EIC and mostly from Dr. V. Eugene Vivian at Conservation Environmental Studies Center were put into play when I taught in a summer program for incoming high school students at Marine Academy of Technology and Environmental Science in Manahawkin, New Jersey.

—Cathy O'Leary, née Reres, retired science teacher,
naturalist and eco-champion, age sixty-nine,
personal communication, January 30, 2024

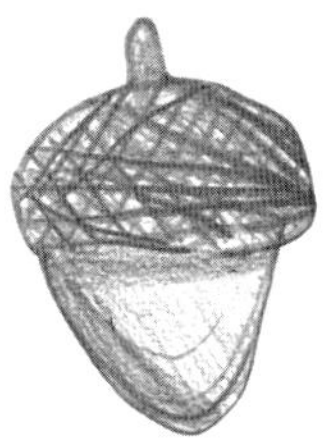

Acorn artwork in this chapter was done by Vayda Beck, age ten, grade five, of the Lacey Township New Jersey Cedar Creek Elementary School.

Epilogue

ENVIRONMENTAL EDUCATION TURNS INTO ENVIRONMENTAL LITERACY AND LEGACY

If we want children to flourish, to become truly empowered, then let us allow them to love the earth before we ask them to save it.

—Beyond Ecophobia: Reclaiming the Heart in Nature Education, *by David Sobel*

Dr. V. Eugene Vivian (May 1, 1915–August 16, 2008)

Once a North Jerseyan, always a North Jerseyan. You can take the boy out of the city, but you can't take the city out of the boy! He died at the age of ninety-three years young on August 16, 2008, in Edgewater, just eight years after fully retiring from an active life of teaching (having formally retired in 1979) and his environmental consulting firm, Associates for Conservation and Environmental Studies (from which he formally retired in 2001). In 2001, he also lost his third wife. In his words, you can feel the love they had for each other: "This was an insurmountable loss. We owed each other so much, now only payable in words. Together we saw and enjoyed much beauty and grand sights. Now whenever I enjoy any experience, I always feel sad that neither of us can any longer enjoy this together. On June 13, 2001, Marie died."

Yet Doc was not someone to be alone for too long, being used to having a big family and constant companionship. A few years after Marie passed, Doc found love again: an old acquaintance and his biographer, Rae Walton-Vivian, née Rasmussen, who cowrote the book *The Ancestry of Vincent Eugene*

Danelle and Chloe Lewis exploring the old Blue Comet railroad tracks in the Pines.
Author's collection.

Ever the explorer, no matter what age: Doc crossing a stream on a log at Whitesbog Village, March 1980. *Courtesy O'Leary family.*

Vivian. They were married on July 31, 2004. Doc and Rae (1921–2019) resided at the time in Little Egg Harbor Township, Ocean, New Jersey. Together they would move back to the region that helped mold Doc in his younger years, to North Jersey.

We know Elizabeth Coleman White's figure in history has overshadowed the men who came before and after her. In 2024, White was inducted into the New Jersey Hall of Fame (NJHOF), in the category Education and Science, and rightfully so—an interesting turning of the page of our history. Lest we forget, another formidable candidate for the NJHOF, Professor Emeritus Dr. V. Eugene Vivian, fits rather nicely into the category of Education and Science, too.

If any among us are to take charge of defending another woman, it's fitting that many of those fighting for our Earth Mother are of the female persuasion. Retired director of Ocean County Parks and Recreation Michael T. Mangum said in a personal interview, "One of the biggest changes at the Parks is that it used to be all men; now it's a few men and mostly women at the Parks." Perhaps as the power dynamic shifts and the past model of patriarchy sunsets, the new rising sun will be women and men together, hand in hand, raising our children and educating them in a village full of love for both space and place. *Atlantic* reporter Alia Wong wrote in a February 20, 2019 article titled "The U.S. Teaching Population Is Getting Bigger, and More Female," "During the 1980–81 school year, roughly two in three—67 percent—public-school teachers were women; by the 2015–16 school year, the share of women teachers had grown to more than three in four, at 76 percent"—echoing what locally in New Jersey and across the United States we are seeing in teaching positions. Naturalists and teachers are the same whether in front of an audience of one or one hundred.

At the 27th Annual Barnegat Bay Environmental Education Roundtable in 2024, the keynote presentation, "Sustainability in Education: Empowering Students to Build a Greener World," was given by Shaina Brenner, a second-grade teacher at Elms Elementary School. "In April of 2023, Elms Elementary was awarded a 10k grant from Sustainable Jersey for Schools to fund Brenner's plan for an Outdoor Environmental Learning Center and Garden"—leaves of hope for a better and greener world, inspiring and leading by example. Looking back to 1973, Doc wrote, "Students in the middle grades, secondary schools, and colleges should be encouraged to take positive action to reflect their own environmental decisions—decisions made hopefully with the benefit of ecological knowledge and wisdom." What would he say to Shaina Brenner's plan for an Outdoor Environmental Learning Center in Jackson, New Jersey? And if he heard another guest at the roundtable, young New Jersey Honey Queen Katie Culbert, speak passionately about a bill sponsored by Senator Linda R. Greenstein to promote the use of native plants for the good of both humankind and the pollinators of the state, what would he say? One can assume: "Bravo! Bravo! Bravo!"

Move over, social media influencers and Hollywood stars. There should be plenty of room for men and women of the environmental movement to be placed in the same space as the more publicly known idols, icons, heroes and heroines, stars and leaders to emulate. Let the names of Rachel Carson, Dr. Eugene "Doc" Vivian, Henry David Thoreau and Shaina and Katie, regardless of sex, race or religion, be known to both young and old as people who strived to put the Earth first and themselves last. Remember: it takes a village, and a community of these types of people is what we want our future generations to be familiar with and to emulate.

If we look at nature's web, specifically in the New Jersey Pinelands National Reserve, our nation's first national reserve, in our mind's eye, a lesson plan unfolds yearly. If we were to write it up, perhaps we'd call it *A Teacher's Guide: The New Jersey Pine Barrens and Fire*. The 1.1 million acres of today wouldn't be without fire. From the ashes, the fire-resistant vegetation rises to grow tall once again. Dominating trees from a hardwood forest that consists of several species of oak tree, silver and red

Opposite and above: Whitesbog Village Water Tower, February 4, 2024. *Author's collection.*

maples and beech trees would replace the pitch pine and scrub oak forests that make up the Pinelands if it weren't for fire, both wild and prescribed burns. Like the environmental teaching landscape, where one generation passes, allowing a new generation to be born, the mighty oaks give way to less dominant trees, creating a magical and one-of-a-kind landscape.

The battle for Mother Earth continues. National, state and municipality-level entities, whether governmental, private or nonprofit organizations, are helping plug the holes or reweave the web in places where our species tore it down. The rural countryside, based in agriculture, once depended on large families, including children's labor, to harvest the crops. Consequently, many children had little time for formal schooling in the early part of the twentieth century. Fast-forward to Dr. Vivian's lifetime in the latter half of the century, when the children weren't working the land; the land was being used to work the children's minds, positively influencing their way of thinking, harking back to a nostalgic attachment to open space and farmland caused by humankind's migration from the farm field to urban environments.

Doc "truly loved the Pine Barrens and was responsible for introducing tens of thousands of schoolchildren to the beauty and mystery of this wondrous region," said Michelle Byers (as quoted in the *Asbury Park Press* on August 19, 2008).

In today's business world, driven by results and data points, it's hard to compare environmental education output to a factory's output. The seed is planted, but for generations, there might not be a sprout. Helping Hands sustains a collective effort to educate the public about the environment. Environmental awareness leads to ecoaction; as Dr. Vivian put it, "A democratic society draws its strength from the participation of as many as possible of its members. The achievement of environmental quality in particular requires the influence of a large number of informed citizens."

Dr. Gallia, a self-proclaimed protege of Dr. Vivian in the 1960s and '70s and vice president emeritus of Rowan University (retired after forty-six years) had some thoughts on the success of people like Doc and his long list of peers (including himself):

> *You can't come up with a final analysis because it's ongoing. I don't think science education as a field absorbed all the things that came out of the environmental movement of the '60s and '70s. I think some things influenced the curriculum, but I couldn't say it was successful. I don't think it was a failure, but I don't think it was successful. Because if you look at the outcomes in terms of pollution and degradation of the environment,*

we are still faced with those problems. The problems were not solved. We are still struggling with that, and it has to deal with a conflict of values. Those people think of themselves as conquering the environment, using the environment to advance their agenda: the environment is there for man's manipulation and taking. Frederick Elder wrote a book, Crisis in Eden, *published in 1970 and referred to them as exclusionists.*

Then there are stewards of the environment, the inclusionists. We are only here for a short time; we need to maintain it, care for it and nurture it. And we are part of it. We need to cherish it in such a way that it is preserved and maintained. We refer to ourselves as inclusionists. Those two things are on the opposite ends of the spectrum. The world is somewhere in between the two. The needle moves back and forth between the two extremes. Today, we're not where we were before in terms of our commitment to environmental issues.

We can only hope for sustained winds. What will the future rallying call be that mirrors the efforts of the 1970s and that decade's first Earth Day, in 1970, which Doc called the "signal year for environmental education"? Is it this year and climate change or maybe the next big thing down the road? Do we do nothing and just wait for a sign or a signal? Perhaps Friends of the Earth, addressing the Stockholm Conference: Only One Earth in 1972, said it best:

Thus in the complex world of living things everything depends on everything else, all life is the same life, every effect is a cause, nothing can happen by itself. You can never do just one thing: the effects of what you do in the world will always spread out like ripples in a pond, and will make faraway and long-delayed changes you have never thought about. Yet you can never do nothing either, for you too are part of the web. Doing just as you have always done is itself doing something, and this too has effects.

A Call to Action (CTA)

1. Find out more about the efforts of local, state and national-level environmental educators. Read what they are doing and why. Seek out the mission statements of organizations defined in this book as "tree nurseries." Maybe you or someone you know will want to become more involved in

those nurseries. Steven Carty once wrote, "We can either swim together or drown apart. We cannot save ourselves; we can only save each other." He was writing about New Jersey's Lenape Indians in vol. 1 of his 2016 zine *My Native Soil: A Journey on Foot from Mount Holly to Tuckerton*, but it's great food for thought concerning environment education and environmental literacy.

2. Call your state and federal legislators and ask them to bring back to full strength or reinvent fully funded programs to sustain environmental learning centers across the country. The work done in the Pinelands Experience at Pinelands Regional High School and at Mount Misery Pinelands Center, New Jersey School of Conservation (SOC) and the CESC at Whitesbog Village is still needed. David Sobel said it best when he wrote in his 2004 book *Place-Based Education: Connecting Classrooms and Communities*, "Place-based education takes us back to basics, but in a broader and more inclusive fashion. Desirable environmental education, or what we're calling place-based education, teaches about both the natural and built environments." And the New Jersey Pinelands National Reserve has many avenues of approach to place-based education. It's another benefit of preserving the Pines. You need it, I need it and the world needs it!

3. If you know of a funding source, whether public, private or taxpayer-supported, find out how we can maximize our collective effort to support the web of oak trees. Let's put our money where our mouth is! A good start would be for Congress to pass something like the 2023 No Child Left Inside Act, which supports environmental education and environmental literacy for our youth!

4. Look to see yourself as a mighty oak like the ones outlined in the chapters of this book. Find an environmental leader whom you can emulate or pick up where they left off. Most importantly, acknowledge the people who make an impact, on yourself or others, and let them know how they make you feel. Authors Saylan and Blumstein are of the opinion that we should drop the term *environmentalism* from our lexicon due to its public image being tarnished. I say that with a little bit of grit and spit, it can shine again. For we know there are more Doc Vivians out there!

Sincerely,
William J. Lewis

Appendix A

THE PINE BARRENS HALL OF FAME

In Bob Birdsall's book *People of the Pines*, published by Plexus Publishing in 2007, he writes,

> *In 2004, in partnership with Plexus Publishing, Inc., Pinelands Preservation Alliance (PPA) created the Pine Barrens Hall of Fame, instituting an annual award. According to Carleton Montgomery, PPA's executive director, "The award was created to honor individuals who, through dedication and hard work, have made a lasting contribution to New Jersey Pinelands Preservation."*

From 2004 to 2014, two governors, Governor Florio and Governor Byrne, were recognized. And in the same year, two individuals of importance to our story were recognized. It was in 2007 that both the son of Dr. Vivian, George Young, and a friend and coworker of Dr. Vivian's, Terry O'Leary, were inducted. The complete list that follows is pulled from the Pinelands Preservation Alliance (PPA) website for your reading pleasure. You can also find it online at https://pinelandsalliance.org/our-work/pine-barrens-hall-of-fame.

2014 Hall of Fame Inductees

Dave Moore *is a visionary and a pioneer in the effort to protect land in New Jersey. He has helped create organizations like New Jersey Future, the Association of New Jersey Environmental Commissions, the Highlands Coalition and the Pinelands Preservation Alliance. He served as Director of the New Jersey Conservation Foundation (NJCF) from 1969 to 1999. During his tenure over 77,000 acres were preserved as public open space. Under his leadership, NJCF was also a major force behind the Pinelands Protection Act, the Freshwater Wetlands Protection Act, Coastal Area Facility Review Act, State Planning Act, Highlands Water Protection and Planning Act and others. Dave is a founding PPA board member and served as chair from 2000 to 2014.*

Michael Catania *has been involved in the preservation, restoration or stewardship of more than 65,500 acres throughout the Garden State. He began his career as an attorney with the Office of Legislative Services where he drafted many of New Jersey's conservation and environmental laws including the Pinelands Protection Act. As state director of the Nature Conservancy in New Jersey, he was instrumental in the protection of thousands of acres in the Pinelands National Reserve. More recently he played a key role in the protection of the 4,200-acre Lenape Farms in Egg Harbor Township. Michael currently serves as executive director of Duke Farms in Hillsborough, NJ.*

2012 Hall of Fame Inductees

A graduate of Rutgers University and a past president of the Philadelphia Botanical Society (1988–2000), Ted Gordon *is a leading authority on the habitats and flora of the New Jersey Pine Barrens. Ted has more than 35 years' experience in botanical studies, including contributions to major plant studies of endangered species in the Pinelands. Ted conducts rare species surveys and research, monitors habitats, and designs management plans for the conservation and enhancement of rare plants. Since 1990, Ted has been an instructor in the Rutgers University Short Course, teaching wetland plant species identification to professional consultants. After chairing the Forestry Advisory Committee of the Pinelands*

Commission for ten years, Ted served as a Pinelands Commissioner from 1999 to 2002.

Jeanne Woodford *and her mother, Elizabeth "Betty" Woodford, began rehabilitating wildlife when a baby great horned owl was dropped off at their Medford home. It wasn't long before the Woodfords' kitchen turned into a wildlife hospital that eventually became Woodford Cedar Run Wildlife Refuge. After her mother's death Jeanne took over management of the Refuge and in 1997 she was able to permanently preserve the 170 acres of prime Pine Barrens habitat where the Refuge resides. Saving the Refuge for wildlife is perhaps Jeanne's greatest accomplishment. Today Cedar Run is the largest wildlife rehabilitation center in the region caring for nearly 4,000 injured or abandoned wild animals and their Education Center provides environmental education to over 20,000 children and adults each year.*

2010 Hall of Fame Inductees

Richard J. Sullivan's *impact on New Jersey's environmental resources cannot be overstated. He has been described by some as the "dean of New Jersey environmentalists." Richard was New Jersey's first commissioner of the Department of Environmental Protection and was the second chairman of the Pinelands Commission, serving for ten years. Former Executive Director of the Pinelands Commission Terrence Moore said, "Richard is one of the most respected public officials this State has been fortunate to have in its government. His sense of fair play, integrity, and commitment to safeguarding our environmental resources continually earns admiration from all with whom he works."*

Betty Wilson *has devoted most of her career to serving the public, and much of that work has been dedicated to protecting the Pinelands and New Jersey's environment. From 1976 to 1980, Betty served as Assistant Commissioner for Regional Projects and then First Deputy Commissioner of the Department of Environmental Protection (DEP). In the late 1980s Betty was engaged by the New Jersey Conservation Foundation as a consultant to assist with the creation of an advocacy group for the Pinelands, resulting in the formation of the Pinelands Preservation Alliance*

(PPA). Betty was appointed to the Pinelands Commission by Governor McGreevey in 2002. In 2005 Governor Codey appointed Betty Chair of the Commission, a position she held until she stepped down in 2008.

2010 Honorees in Education: *Terry Loy of Woodford Cedar Run Wildlife Refuge and Susan Girard of Burlington County College's PINES program were also honored.*

2008 Hall of Fame Inductees

Dr. David Fairbrother's *diverse body of work has had a tremendous impact on the preservation of flora in the state of New Jersey. Dr. Fairbrothers is Professor Emeritus and former chair of the Department of Biological Sciences at Rutgers University. He also served as Curator of the Chrysler Herbarium from 1954 to 1988. The herbarium's collections of Pinelands flora provided much of the documentation necessary for Congress to establish the Pinelands National Reserve. The collections also provided essential support for the United Nations to designate the Pinelands National Reserve an International Biosphere Reserve in 1983. Dr. Fairbrothers and other researchers used Chrysler Herbarium specimens to produce the first State list of Rare and Endangered Plants in the United States (1973). This publication was significant in helping persuade the United States Congress to enact the first U.S. Endangered Species Act in 1973.*

Dr. Richard T.T. Forman *taught at Rutgers University from 1966 to 1984, where he directed the Botany (and Plant Physiology) Graduate Program for four years and served as Director of the Hutcheson Memorial Forest Center from 1972 to 1984. It was during this time that he edited the book* Pine Barrens: Ecosystem and Landscape. *This book brought together the work of 41 experts who covered topics such as people in the landscape, vegetation, geology, hydrology, animal communities and much more. Published in 1979, the book came out just in time to serve as one of the major resources for the creation of the Pinelands Comprehensive Management Plan, the nation's foremost ecosystem-based land use planning system. The timing was perfect, as the book in its entirety makes the case for the Pine Barrens of New Jersey to be viewed as a landscape. In fact,*

Chapter 33, titled "The Pine Barrens of New Jersey: An Ecological Mosaic" and authored by Dr. Forman, is arguably the original publication of modern landscape ecology.

DR. ROBERT ZAMPELLA *was the first Chief Scientist for New Jersey's Pinelands Commission. During his tenure, Robert developed the Pinelands Commission's science program into a powerhouse of ecological research. The program's scientists have published numerous articles in peer-reviewed science journals, which is unusual for a government agency. Dr. Zampella also played a key role in the development of the original Comprehensive Management Plan (CMP), the regional land use document that governs preservation and development in the Pinelands National Reserve. One of the great strengths of the Pinelands CMP is its firm grounding in environmental science, and Dr. Zampella's work enabled the Pinelands Commission to continue adjusting the CMP in light of the growing body of research on the region's unique ecology and human impacts on the ecosystem.*

2008 HONOREES IN EDUCATION: *Phil Levy, Lacey Township High School and Julie Akers, Cunningham Alternative School in Vineland and a founder of the Great Egg Harbor Watershed Association.*

2007 HALL OF FAME INDUCTEES

NAN HUNTER-WALNUT *was a founding member of the Pine Barrens Coalition, one of the first recognized organizations dedicated to protecting the Pine Barrens ecosystem. In 1977 Governor Brendan Byrne placed a moratorium on development in the Pinelands and established the Pinelands Review Committee to plan and coordinate state actions to protect the Pine Barrens. The Governor selected Nan to work on the task of delineating the Pinelands boundaries for protection during this contentious time. Not one to shy away from her civic responsibilities, Nan was the first woman and the first environmentalist on the planning board for Southampton Township. She served from 1978 to 2003. She was made chairwoman of the planning board after 20 years of service. Nan was a founding board member of the Pinelands Preservation Alliance and was a staunch advocate for preservation before the Pinelands Commission.*

JANET JACKSON-GOULD *spent 20 years as a member of New Jersey Audubon Society's board, three of them as president. During the late 1970s–early 1980s she was an active member of the Pine Barrens Coalition, the leading local citizens' group that worked to protect the Pines through the adoption of the federal and state Pinelands laws. In this capacity, Janet worked with Nan Hunter-Walnut to involve the public, gain publicity and pressure the politicians to bring the dream of protecting the Pinelands to reality. Janet was curator of education at the Philadelphia Zoo for twelve years, founding director of Outside-In, the children's museum at the Academy of Natural Sciences of Philadelphia, and assistant director of the Please Touch Museum. Janet served first as a volunteer and then as executive director of the Woodford Cedar Run Wildlife Refuge in Medford.*

COL. ELMER C. ROWLEY, USMRC, *grew up in the High Sierras of California. Elmer was commissioned in the US Marine Corps in 1935 and served in active duty and the reserves until 1973. In 1962 Elmer, his wife, Thelma, and their two sons moved to Centennial Pines in Medford. They fell in love with the Pine Barrens. In the mid-1960s Elmer joined the Pine Barrens Conservationists, one of the first recognized organizations dedicated to protecting the Pine Barrens ecosystem. Elmer was a strong and tireless advocate for the Pine Barrens in his capacity as a board member of the New Jersey Audubon Society and later as board president from 1973 to 1975. When Elmer joined the board of NJAS, he quickly became the Society's lead spokesman for Pinelands preservation. He took the message to the nation's capital, attending several committee meetings of the U.S. House and Senate as a representative of NJAS.*

2007 HONOREES IN EDUCATION: *George Young, Terry O'Leary, Christine Raabe*

2006 HALL OF FAME INDUCTEES

FRANKLIN PARKER *was appointed the first Chair of the Pinelands Commission in 1979 by Governor Brendan Byrne. It was not an easy assignment. Bitterly opposed by some communities and leaders, the Pinelands Protection Act required the Commission to develop and adopt a comprehensive land use management plan for over 1 million acres of the nation's most crowded state—a plan that would preserve and enhance the region's unique natural resources, while also allowing compatible development and protecting a deeply embedded agricultural tradition. Beryl Robichaud Collins described Frank at this time as "a low-key individual with an unusual ability to defuse highly politicized situations and to steer group deliberations constructively on complex issues." It is a tribute to Frank's leadership that the Commission ultimately voted 11 to 4 in favor of adopting the Plan, which radically changed the way land is regulated in almost ¼ of the state of New Jersey. Frank served as Chair of the Commission until 1988, working with Terry Moore and other Commissioners to ensure continuity during the Plan's first decade.*

In 1979, Terrence C. Moore *was appointed by Governor Brendan Byrne as the first Executive Director of the New Jersey Pinelands Commission. During his tenure, the Commission was constituted, the Comprehensive Management Plan was written and adopted, and the Pinelands Commission implemented the Plan through 20 sometimes turbulent years. Under Terry's guidance, the Plan incorporated a truly regional vision and deployed a wide range of strategies such as municipal conformance, a strong transferable development rights program, protection of threatened and endangered species habitats, rigorous scientific monitoring and density transfer mechanisms. Terry became famous for his dry humor, his skill at diffusing tense situations at public meetings over the Commission's work, and his extraordinary ability to get (at least) the "8 votes" needed for the Commission to take action. With Terry's leadership, the Pinelands Plan won general acceptance and support over the years. Terry served as the Commission's Executive Director from 1979 to 1999.*

2005 Hall of Fame Inductees

Brendan T. Byrne *served as Governor of New Jersey from 1974 to 1982. He had many accomplishments as Governor. Foremost among these in the minds of many was the passage of the Pinelands Protection Act and the launching of the Pinelands Commission and Comprehensive Management Plan. As Governor, Brendan Byrne led the effort to save the Pinelands. From the beginning of these efforts, he and his administration worked to create a strong regional planning agency and a regional plan based on the fundamental goal of protecting the Pinelands' natural resources. While pressing for passage of the Pinelands Protection Act, Gov. Byrne issued Executive Order 71, a bold measure that imposed a moratorium on development over a vast area until the Pinelands Comprehensive Management Plan could be adopted. Gov. Byrne appointed the first Chair of the Pinelands Commission, Franklin Parker, and its first Executive Director, Terry Moore, providing the Commission with the leadership it needed to institute the groundbreaking development control measures embodied in the Comprehensive Management Plan.*

Jim Florio *served three terms in the New Jersey General Assembly and in 1974, he was elected to Congress to represent the 1st District of New Jersey. During this time, then Congressman Florio introduced legislation to create a 970,000-acre Pine Barrens Ecological Reserve. This bill evolved into what became Section 502 of the National Parks and Recreation Act of 1978, the federal legislation that created the Pinelands National Reserve and set out the principles on which the region's natural resources should be protected through a comprehensive land use management plan. The following year, New Jersey adopted the Pinelands Protection Act of 1979, which fulfilled the goals of the federal legislation by creating the Pinelands Commission and charging it with writing and implementing the Pinelands Comprehensive Management Plan. During his years in Congress, he also authored the act popularly known as the "Superfund" law, our nation's primary program for cleaning up hazardous waste sites. Jim Florio was elected Governor of New Jersey in 1990. As Governor, he carried his concern with environmental protection into his administration. In addition to many important reforms, he was responsible for signing into law the Clean Water Enforcement Act, one of the strongest laws of its type in the nation.*

2005 Honorees in Education: *Maureen Barrett, Richard Prickett*

2004 Hall of Fame Inductees

An entomologist, botanist, editor, teacher, photographer, filmmaker, writer, and naturalist, Howard P. Boyd *had a close association with the Pine Barrens of New Jersey spanning more than 65 years. In 1969, after 31 years as an executive with the Boy Scouts of America, he retired, and had very successful careers as an author and in entomology. He was considered one of the world's leading experts on tiger beetles. Three of Howard's books have helped raise awareness of the Pinelands ecosystem both regionally and nationally.* A Field Guide to the Pine Barrens of New Jersey *is recognized as the most authoritative and widely referenced field guide to New Jersey Pinelands flora and fauna. His other books are* A Pine Barrens Odyssey: A Naturalist's Year in the Pine Barrens of New Jersey, Wildflowers of the Pine Barrens of New Jersey, *and* The Ecological Pine Barrens of New Jersey: An Ecosystem Threatened by Fragmentation.

BERYL ROBICHAUD COLLINS *was best known in the Pinelands region as the author and editor of important works on the history of the Pinelands protection movement and the natural resources of New Jersey. With Emily Russell, Beryl edited and wrote much of* Protecting the New Jersey Pinelands: A New Direction in Land-Use Management *(Rutgers University Press, 1988), the bible and indispensable reference on the extraordinary sequence of events leading to the adoption of the Pinelands Protection Act and Comprehensive Management Plan. With Karl Anderson, Beryl wrote the highly regarded* Plant Communities of New Jersey: A Study in Landscape Diversity *(Rutgers University Press, 1994). Both books remain in print and continue to provide a rich source of information and inspiration for conservationists both regionally and nationally. As a researcher at Rutgers University, she was a key member of a team of scientists who helped spur national recognition of the Pinelands' unique natural resources thereby shaping the course of the federal and state Pinelands protection program. Beryl authored* A Conceptual Framework for Pinelands Decision-Making for the Pinelands Commission, *a source for several basic resource protection strategies now embodied in the Pinelands Comprehensive Management Plan.*

2004 HONOREES IN EDUCATION: *Dayna Mennen (Angelozzi), Ron Smith, John Volpa*

Appendix B

PINELANDS COALITION PAMPHLET

WHAT ARE THE PINE BARRENS' RESOURCES?

PRISTINE GROUNDWATER: Seventeen trillion gallons of the purest drinking water in the nation.

FARMING: Twenty-four per cent of the state's agricultural income, especially cranberry, blueberry and shellfishing industries.

RECREATION: Hunting, fishing, cycling, canoeing on the Wild and Scenic Rivers, hiking, camping and swimming. The forty-mile Batona Hiking Trail is entirely in the Pine Barrens.

THE WILDERNESS: Vast pine, oak and cedar woodlands. The Dwarf Forest, known all over the world. Some endangered plant and animal species exist nowhere else on earth.

CULTURE: Native lifestyle, music, crafts.

HISTORY: Important historical and archeological sites throughout region.

A NATIONALLY AND INTERNATIONALLY UNIQUE AREA

THE PINE BARRENS COALITION

MEMBER ORGANIZATIONS

American Youth Hostels, Delaware Valley Council
American Littoral Society
American Rivers Conservation Council
Appalachian Mountain Club, New York
Association of New Jersey Environmental Commissions
Atlantic Ocean Alliance
Audubon Society, Bucks County, Pennsylvania
Audubon Society, Jersey Shore
Audubon Wildlife Society
Batona Hiking Club
BBB Hunting Club
Big Timer Creek/Cooper River Watershed Association
Burlington County Natural Sciences Club
Cape May County Environmental Council
Cherry Hill Environmental Action Committee
Cape May County Environmental Defense Fund
Citizens Association for Protection of the Environment
Citizens Conservation Council of Ocean County
Citizens Conservation Council, Laurel Springs
Committee for a Better Environment
Concerned Citizens of Tabernacle Township
Concerned Citizens of Woodland Township
Cumberland County Conservation League
Delran Environmental Advisory Agency
Florence Association of Concerned Townspeople
Friends of the Earth
Friends of the Rancocas
Great Egg Harbor River Association
League for Conservation Legislation
Mid-Pine Barrens Watershed Association
Metropolitan Canoe and Kayak Club, New York
Nature Conservancy
New Jersey Audubon Society
New Jersey Conservation Foundation
New Jersey Public Interest Research Group
Outdoor Club of South Jersey
Pine Barrens Conservationists
Pompeston Creek Watershed Association
Project U.S.E.
Rancocas Creek Watershed Association
River Touring Group, New York
Safe Energy Alternatives Alliance
Serious Taxpayers Opposed to Pollution
Short Hills Garden Club
South Jersey Federation of Environmentalists
Stockton Volunteers for the Environment
West Chester Bird Club, Pennsylvania
Whiting Protect Our Pines
Wilderness Society
Youth Environmental Society
Friends

SUPPORTING ORGANIZATIONS

Environmental Defense Fund
Natural Resources Defense Council
Sierra Club
National Parks and Conservation Association
The National Audubon Society

Appendix B: New Jersey Pine Barrens Coalition pamphlet. *Courtesy O'Leary family.*

Appendix C

V. EUGENE VIVIAN, PhD, RECORD OF EDUCATION AND EXPERIENCE

RECORD OF EDUCATION AND EXPERIENCE

V. E .Vivian, Ph.D. Resumé

V. Eugene Vivian, Ph.D.
Address: 284 Country Club Blvd.
Little Egg Harbor, NJ 08087
Home Phone: 609-296-7479
FAX: 609-296-1233
Birthdate:May 12, 1915

I. **EDUCATION**

American University, Washington,DC, 1964
University of Montana, Boseman,1960 Post doctoral studies - funded by National Science Foundation New York University, 1946–1958 (part-time) Ph.D.,1958 Thesis: ***Scientific Principles Underlying the Conservation of Soils, Forests and Grassland.***
Paterson State College, NJ, 1945 – graduate study
School of Pharmacy, Columbia University, 1943, 1944 – graduate study
Montclair State College, NJ, 1942 – graduate study
Columbia University Graduate School of Science, 1937–1941, M.A.1940 – Botany
Montclair State College, NJ, B.A. 1936 (majors in biology, chemistry; minors in Physics and English)
Summer Sessions, Montclair State College 1935, 1936
Paterson State College, NJ, 1932–1933
Eastside High School, Paterson, NJ, high school diploma, 1932

II. **PROFESSIONAL EXPERIENCE**

President, Associates for Conservation & Environmental Studies, 1984–2000
Professor Emeritus, Glassboro State College, 1979 to present
Professor of Science and Environmental Studies, Glassboro State College, 1955–1979
Executive Director, Conservation and Environmental Studies Center, Inc., an independent non-profit corporation providing 21 special environmental consultation services for public and private agencies, beginning February 1, 1971–December 1984
Director CCSS National Science Foundation Grant in Ecology and Environmental Studies for Elementary School Teachers at Glassboro State College, 1971–1972
Director Conservation and Environmental Studies Center, funded as a Title III project in 1966 for a planning grant with the School District of Glassboro under the Elementary-Secondary Education Act, and for a consortium of 70 school districts and Glassboro School District, 1968–1971
Director, Experienced Teacher Fellowship Program in Environmental Education, Glassboro, Montclair and Trenton State Colleges, 1967–69

Director CCSS National Science Foundation Grant in elementary school science (SCIS) at Glassboro State College, 1968–69
Chairman, Department of Science, Glassboro State College, Glassboro, NJ, 1955–1967
Post Doctoral Research, National Science Foundation, Highlands Biological Station, North Carolina, Summers 1961, 1962, 1963, Spring 1964
Visiting Professor, University of Utah, Summer 1960
Adjunct Professor of Physical Science, Rutgers University, 1951; 1955–1960
Director, Audio Visual Education, Miami Beach High, Florida, 1955
Associate Professor Sciences, State College, Paterson, NJ, 1945–1955
Chemistry Instructor - part time, 1942–1945
Director, Camp Deer Trail, Herald Tribune Fresh Air Fund Camp, Summer 1947
Director of Camping and Research, Herald Tribune Fresh Air Fund, 1950/51 (on leave of absence from Paterson State College, Paterson, NJ)
Visiting Staff Member, National Camp (Camp Leadership Training Center) of Life Camps, Inc., 1947–50
Science Teacher, Paterson Eastside High School, 1939–1945
Science Teacher, Park Ridge High School, 1936–1939

III. **PUBLICATIONS IN BOOKS**

Vivian, V. Eugene and Thomas T. Rillo. "Focus on Environmental Education" The Curriculum Development Council for Southern New Jersey, R. Simone Ed., Glassboro State College, NJ, 1970.

Vivian, V.E. *"Sourcebook for Environmental Education"*, Mosby-Times Mirror, St. Louis, 1973.

Vivian,V.E. "Ecology for Children", *Air,Water,Land Plants and Animals*, DPR Publishers, Newfield, NJ, 1975.

Snyder, D.B. and V.E. Vivian. *"Rare and Endangered Vascular Plants of New Jersey"*, U.S. Fish and Wildlife Service, Newton Corner, MA, 1982.

IV. **SPECIAL PUBLICATIONS**

Vivian, V.E. *"Intermediate Math - Metric"*, DPR Publishers, Newfield, NJ, 1974.

Vivian, V.E. et al. *Master Plan and Natural Resource Inventory for Bass River Township, NJ,* Burlington County, NJ., The Conservation and Environmental Studies Center, Browns Mills, NJ, 1982.

Vivian, V.E.*"Habitat Investigations on Threatened Plant Species in the New Jersey Pine Barrens and their implications in Natural and Cultural Resources of the New Jersey Pine Barrens"*, Stockton State College, Pomona, NJ, J.W. Sinton, Ed., 1978.

Vivian, V.E., Principal Investigator, *Wetlands Faunal Study*, Passaic River Basin, prepared by Conservation and Environmental Studies Center for U.S. Fish and Wildlife Service and the New York District U.S. Army Corps of Engineers, March 1980.

V. **PUBLICATIONS IN PERIODICALS**

Vivian,V.Eugene and Ernest E. Henderson. "Environmental Education", Instructor Magazine, January, 1972.

Vivian, V. Eugene. "Science in the Outdoor Laboratory" New Jersey Science Teachers Association Bulletin, Volume 17, No. 3, January, 1969.

______"The Ecological Life History of Shortia galacifolia, Bulletin of Torrey Botanical Club, 1967.

______"Science is Asking", New Jersey Education Review, November, 1966.

______"Let's Really Put Nature Back in our Camping Programs", Camping Magazine, Winter, 1952.

______"A Key to the Buds and Twigs of Northern New Jersey", The New Jersey Science Teacher, Oct.1950.

______"Symmetry in Sagina", Bulletin of Torrey Botanical Club, December, 1941 (publication of master's thesis).

VI. **PROFESSIONAL ORGANIZATIONS**

American Association for the Advancement of Science
American Biology Teachers Association
American Camping Association
American Forestry Association
Association for the Education of Teachers in Science
Association of Health, Physical Education and Recreation
Association of New Jersey State College Faculties
Conservation Education Association
Delaware Valley Clean Air Council - Board of Directors - 1967–1971
Friends of the Land
Geological Society of New Jersey, Charter member and Treasurer, 1958–1960
Glassboro State College Faculty Association - President - 1965–1967
Gloucester County Citizens Association, Vice-President, 1965–1967
Kappa Delta Pi-Beta Pi Chapter - Honorary Education Fraternity
National Association for Research in Science Teaching

National Education Association
National Science Teachers Association (Life Member)
New Jersey Academy of Science
New Jersey Education Association
New Jersey Science Teachers Association
New Jersey State Council for Environmental Education–Council Member
New York - New Jersey Trail Conference
Southern New Jersey Association for Science Education - Founder - 1959
Torrey Botanical Club
New Jersey Outdoor Education Association - President - 1965–1967
Association of Wetland Scientists

VII. **HONORS - CITATIONS**

Founder's Day Award, New York University 1959 – for scholarship.
New Jersey Conservation Educator of the Year - 1967 - New Jersey State Federation of Sportmen's Clubs in cooperation with the National Wildlife Federation and the Sears & Roebuck Foundation National Conservation Educator of the year - 1968 - National Wildlife Federation.
Citation - New Jersey Science Teachers Association for outstanding service and achievement in Resource Conservation in the field of Education, 1969.
Citation - Soil Conservation Society of America - 1970 - for outstanding service and achievement in Resource Conservation in the field of Education.
Arbor Day Award, Stafford Township, Year's Theme "Trees Against Pollution" or TAP April 2000 Tree planted in Dr. Vivian's honor, a Sweet Gum.
Eugene Vivian Environmental Education Scholarship for a graduate student at Rowan University each year starting September 2001.
Eugene Vivian Director's Office designated at Camp Tommy (formerly Camp Pioneer) NY Fresh Air Fund Dedication 17 July 2001.

VIII. **PUBLIC SERVICE/PROFESSIONAL RESPONSIBILITIES**

NJ Department of Environmental Protection, Pinelands Commission - Educational Advisory Council, Speaker's Bureau Ocean County, NJ.
Member, Advisory Council for Cattus Island Environmental Center, Ocean County Parks & Recreation Department.
Township of Little Egg Harbor, NJ – Environmental Commission, Chairperson 1983–1999.

Appendix C: Dr. Vivian's résumé. *Courtesy George and Nadine Young.*

Appendix D

EXPLOITATION OF THE PINE BARRENS PAST, PRESENT AND FUTURE

Authored by Frank G. Patterson, with contributions and editing by Norma T. Vivian. Pictured are the last three pages of this 1969 CESC publication.

LAND DEVELOPMENT

PAST, PRESENT AND FUTURE

Land in the Pine Barrens has changed hands many times. Often the land was promoted as offering good homesites or as investment property. The ownership of some land is in doubt, since some deeds were never recorded. There have been 400 lands development schemes involving 200,000 acres, 1,000,000 persons and $100,000,000.

The most famous of the land schemes was Paisley, "The Magic City" which consisted of 1,400 acres of land between Chatsworth and Tabernacle which were bought for $5,146 in 1898. Approximately 80% of the land was too sandy to support crops, lawns or gardens, but lots were sold with glowing inducements and promises. Only twelve houses and one store were built in Paisley; none of these exist today.

Large acreage in the Pine Barrens is in private or corporate ownership, being held for profit or development. The owner of 5,000 acres near Chatsworth wants to develop an industrial park. Real estate syndicates offer building lots for sale, but without the false promises of another Paisley. In many areas, housing developments are being built especially around abandoned cranberry bogs which have been deepened – reflooded to create a lake. On smaller plots of land, usually alongside roads, can be found single homes and smaller businesses.

Present and Future Plans

In an effort to avoid the haphazard development of the Pine Barrens, a Pinelands Regional Planning Board was formed, consisting of representatives of Burlington and Ocean counties. The Board suggested five different plans for future developments, and on June 10, 1965, they adopted the following plan for a Jetport – New City proposal:

1. Roadways –
   a. construction of Rt. 33 from Trenton to Toms River, with approximately 15 miles in the Pine Barrens;
   b. construction of Rt. 38 from Camden to Asbury Park crossing the northern section of the Pine Barrens;
   c. construction of a Garden State Parkway link south of Toms River and Point Pleasant with access to the Jetport or New City;
   d. dualization of Rt. 72 to connect Rt. 70 with the shore points and to facilitate access to the Jetport from Trenton and New York City;
   e. dualization of Rt. 206 in the western area of the Pine Barrens, also county route 539;
   f. relocation and reconstruction of other county roads may be included.

2. Location of a 32,500 acre jetport, larger than Kennedy, LaGuardia, and Newark Airports combined, and a 10,800 acre New City along the parkway link connected with Philadelphia and New York by rail.

3. Expansion of a permanent open space land reserve from 250 square miles in the central portion of the region.

4. Continuation of McGuire Air Force Base, Fort Dix Army Base, and Lakehurst Naval Station.

5. Concentration of urban growth, exclusive of New City, on the periphery of the Pinelands region.

6. Location of major industrial parks, from 200–3,000 acres in size, concentrated in the Jetport – New City area.

Future Land Use

Permanent Open Space	500 square miles
Military Areas	67 " "
Urbanized	236 " "
Jetport	51 " "
New City and Industry	26.5 " "
Large Lot Rural Development, Agricultural	66 " "
	946.5 square miles

The other four alternative plans are:

Alternative One – Low Growth – Corridor. This is the least desirable plan because it is a continuation of present trends with development along present roads.

Alternative Two – High Growth – Scatteration. The advantages of this plan are high economic input with easy implementation. The disadvantages would be too much sprawl with some duplication of services.

Alternative Three – Restricted Growth Scatteration. A chief advantage of this plan would be the permanent establishment of high recreational resources. A disadvantage would be high cost for few services. This assumes establishment of the jetport elsewhere but does not preclude later construction. It suggests that all state owned lands be joined together and all development limited to the periphery

Alternative Four – Jetport – New Towns. The advantages of this plan would be high economic use of the land. Disadvantages include high governmental involvement implementation. The new self-contained towns would serve the Jetport.

Another proposal for part of the Pine Barrens is that of the Pine Barrens National Monument Committee which suggests the development of a National Monument of not less than 150,000 acres bordered by Lebanon, Penn, Bass River and Wharton Tract State Forests. It would be operated by the United States Department of the Interior and administered by the National Park Service.

Comparison of Four Alternate Plans Regarding Land Use
And Population Growth as Suggested by the Pinelands Regional Planning Board

	AREA IN SQUARE MILES			
	Alt. 1	Alt. 2	Alt. 3	Alt. 4
ULTIMATE DEVELOPED AREA	150	250	150	200
ULTIMATE OPEN SPACE	600	550	700	500
RURAL DEVELOPMENT	135	85	35	85
MILITARY	65	65	65	65
TOTAL Area In Square Miles	950	950	950	950
1985 POPULATION	100,000	250,000	100,000	200,000

Since the possibility of a jetport in the Pine Barrens for the giant super-jets soon to be added to airline fleets has been introduced, opposition has mounted against such a proposal. In recent years, conservation, wildlife and nature groups have joined with Pine Barrens residents, to protest the wanton destruction such a jetport would impose on the Pine Barrens. Like, Hamlet, "to be or not to be" is the Jetport's question.

The Jetport issue has become a political, as well as personal, issue with thousands of voters. In 1969, voters of Ocean and Burlington Counties answered YES or NO to the question: "Shall the Board of Chosen Freeholders of the County of _______ support the establishment of an international jetport in the south central area of the State of New Jersey?"

The Answer on November 4, 1969 was NO by a margin of 2.4 no to each yes vote.

One proposal for utilizing the Pine Barrens has been initiated and is being developed at Whitesbog (see Agriculture section) by the Conservation and Environmental Science Center (CESC). A staff of practical-minded educators, led by a Glassboro State College professor and former Science Department chairman, Dr. V. Eugene Vivian, believe that the very technological developments that are tearing away at the environment can be manipulated to refurbish it. Working with industry, governmental agencies, colleges and universities, CESC will emphasize research in environmental science as well as implementing environmental education as an integral part of the total curriculum in the schools.

CESC's plans for the Whitesbog site call for an innovative architectural design in harmony with the land to serve as a model center for environmental studies. One such study is the "Conservation and Environmental Renewal and Development Program" for the Pine Barrens Complex. CESC recognizes the Pine Barrens as being the largest single ecological region in New Jersey. With its low population density, abundant water resources and priceless ecological heritage, the Pine Barrens area is New Jersey's greatest opportunity for environmental planning to meet the population and land use challenge of the future.

Appendix D: *Exploitation of the Pine Barrens: Past, Present and Future* by CESC, Inc. *Author's collection.*

Opposite: *Pinelands Preservation Alliance Newsletter* article by Dr. Vivian titled "A Facet in New Jersey's Jewel," circa 1980s. *Author's collection.*

Appendix E

A FACET IN NEW JERSEY'S JEWEL

A Facet in New Jersey's Jewel

by V. Eugene Vivian, Ph.D. - Professor Emeritus, Glassboro State College, Conservation & Environmental Studies Center

The jewel, of course, is New Jersey's Pinelands, under protection by virtue of state and federal legislation. One scintillating facet is the broom crowberry and its habitat, the pygmy forest, more properly known as the pine plains.

Broom crowberry *(Corema conradii)* is a State of New Jersey endangered shrub species which grows no further south than Ocean and Burlington counties. The multi-acre sized patches in which the crowberry is often found make it accessible to anyone who wishes to see it.

The early ecologist, J.W. Harshberger, was so impressed by the crowberry and its manner of growth that he proposed to designate the entire pygmy pine forest formation as the Coremal, but that name never gained favor with other botanists and ecologists. Perhaps you, the reader, will be moved to seek out *Corema* to admire or photograph it. It's easier to locate than the more heralded curly grass fern, and somewhat more photogenic.

More than a hundred years ago the broom crowberry attracted much attention from the botanists of the day. Witmer Stone (1911) devoted more than four pages of description to the broom crowberry; for other species he most commonly accorded a two to three paragraph description in his classic, *Plants of Southern New Jersey.*

Broom or Conrad's Crowberry was named for its discoverer, Solomon W. Conrad, circa 1831. Known only by a handful of botanists until 1854, the plant was lost (not discoverable) until 1884 when it was rediscovered by Columbia College professor F.H.J. Merrill near Cedar Bridge (vicinity of Route 72 and County 539 intersection). Besides being endangered, what's special about it is that it's the first blooming plant in the pines. Only the red maple and the red cedar shed pollen earlier. Occasionally the golden club, pyxie moss and the alder bloom by March 21st, or thereabouts, but the crowberry comes into flowering in acre-sized plots.

In New Jersey, Spring comes last to the Pine Barrens. The cool mountain areas, the warmer interiors and the shore areas all leaf out with abundant flowers long before mid-May, which is coming out time for Pine Barrens trees, shrubs and herbs. I have seen the crowberry in flower as early as March 19th or as late as April 9th. Harshberger (1916) has similar dates in his unique phenology (graphs of flowering and fruiting dates for many pineland species).

Nothing about the broom crowberry is prepossessing or special unless you are in love with it. That is because it is a low evergreen shrub four to six inches high with many quarter inch needles irregularly clustered about the short stems. The leaf edges are rolled under and meet in a light colored line; this produces a tubular appearing leaf.

You could readily mistake the much more ubiquitous Pine Barrens (golden) heather for the broom crowberry. Both shrubs grow in clumps with patches of white sand separating them. In late March the golden heather has a more gray green hue from its short sharp scaly leaves; they and the stems are much more hairy than those of the broom crowberry. If you do run into the golden heather *(Hudsonia eridoides)* it will be rewarding to return in later May to see masses of yellow blossoms atop the white sands. And, if you have learned to recognize the crowberry, you may look for its tiny round golden brown pods.

To visit the broom crowberry most readily, go to Warren Grove on Ocean County Route 539. Just south of the firehouse turn west on Sims Place Road and after less than a mile, turn right (north) on Beaverdam Road. Follow the narrow black-top until you see the Federal Overseas Radio Communication facility accessed by one-car width pavement. What appears to be a mowed lawn is really a mixture of broom crowberry and golden heather.

If you visit on April Fool's Day, the joke won't be on you. Bring a hand magnifier, but leave your shovel at home; it is not transplantable. Kneel in the sand to see flowers in the form of deep wine-red stems at the tips of the short evergreen branches. Don't look for petals; there are none. The slender unmistakable wine-red stalks are the filaments or stems of the pollen bearing organs surmounted by brown anther or pollen sacs.

If this experience has turned out as described, you will have witnessed an unusual sight. Here, the broom crowberry is at the southernmost part of its growth range. Further north, almost always coastal, it can be found in Massachusetts at Plymouth, Cape Cod, Nantucket, on some coastal Maine islands, Canadian Nova Scotia, and Newfoundland. One exception is in Ulster County, New York on the Schunemunk Mountain. I have verified each of these locations except for Newfoundland.

To account for the presence of *Corema* in New Jersey, today's botanists believe that continental glaciation forced it southward with the advance of the ice. The crowberry then followed the retreat of the ice northward about ten thousand years ago.

Fortunately, much of the crowberry habitat is in the Preservation Zone of the Pinelands. The Pinelands Preservation Alliance, and you, it's members, must be continually vigilant to protect and maintain the habitats of all endangered and threatened species in the Pine Barrens. Without them, the facets of the jewel will be extinguished.

BIBLIOGRAPHY

Agency for Toxic Substances and Disease Registry. "DDT, DDE, and DDD: ToxFAQs." https://www.atsdr.cdc.gov/toxfaqs/tfacts35.pdf.

American Camp Association. "Pinelands Center at Mt. Misery: Overnight Camp." https://find.acacamps.org/program_profile.php?program_id=6647.

Ardoin, James. Personal interview with the author. April 15, 2024.

Augustine, Sarah E., Kiyomi E. Locker and Dennis McDonald. *Whitesbog*. Images of America series. Arcadia Publishing, 2022.

Bailey, L.H. *The Nature-Study Idea*. Doubleday, Page, 1903.

Beck, H.C. *Forgotten Towns of Southern New Jersey*. Rutgers University Press, 1961.

Birdsall, Bob. *People of the Pines*. Plexus, 2007.

Blumstein, Daniel T., and Charles Saylan. *The Failure of Environmental Education (And How We Can Fix It)*. University of California Press, 2011

Bolger, William, Herbert J. Githens and Edward S. Rutsch. *Historic Architectural Survey and Preservation Planning Project for the Village of Whitesbog Burlington County, New Jersey*. New Jersey Conservation Foundation, 1982.

Boyd, Howard P. *The Ecological Pine Barrens of New Jersey: An Ecosystem Threatened by Fragmentation*. Plexus, 2008.

———. *A Field Guide to the Pine Barrens of New Jersey: Its Flora, Fauna, Ecology and Historic Sites*. Plexus, 1991.

Boy Scouts of America. *Revised Handbook for Boys*. 1935.

Carlson, Julie. *Never Finished Just Begun: A Narrative History of L.B. Sharp and Outdoor Education*. Beaver's Pond Press, 2009.

Carty, Steven R. *My Native Soil: A Journey on Foot from Mount Holly to Tuckerton. Vol. I: The Shamong Trail*. Self-published, 2016.

CBS. "1970: The First Earth Day in New York City." YouTube. www.youtube.com/watch?v=nEmARFci__I.

Conservation and Environmental Science Center. "Conservation & Environmental Science Center Environmental Education." July 1970.

———. *Local Education Guidebook for Resident Environmental Education Program*. https://files.eric.ed.gov/fulltext/ED033784.pdf.

County Bell. "Whitesbog: N.J. Property in Search of a Plan." September/October/November 1983.

Cunningham, John T. *This Is New Jersey.* Rutgers University Press, 1978.
Duvoisin, Marc. "Restoration Trying to Save Whitesbog from Rotting on the Vine." *Philadelphia Inquirer*, October 3, 1983.
Dwier, Lois Ann. *Wilderness Wetlands in Spring.* Edlo Books, 1983.
Elder, Frederick. *Crisis in Eden.* Abingdon Press, 1970.
Elizabeth Meirs Morgan 1913–2004. Ocean County Historical Society, 2004.
Fallon, Scott, and Amanda Oglesby. "From Superfund Law to Pinelands Protection, Florio Remembered as an Environmental Champion." September 26, 2022. https://www.northjersey.com.
Forked River Gazette. "Hot Off the Press: 'Ye Olde Clamtown Almanac' by Local Author Lee M. Gant." Mid-September 1997.
Forked River Mountain Coalition. http://www.frmc.org.
Friedman, Sally. "Whitesbog Journal; In Abandoned Village, Twofold Restoration." *New York Times*, June 27, 1993.
Friends of the Earth. *Only One Earth: An Introduction to the Politics of Survival.* Earth Island, 1972.
Gallia, Thomas. Personal interview with the author. August 13, 2024.
Gant, Lee M. "Those Picturesque Pinelands." *Reporter*, 1969 to 1975.
Georgieff, German. Personal interview with the author. January 26, 2024.
Gomez, Lillian Hoey. Personal interview with the author. March 15, 2024.
Griffin, Thomas H., Jr. "In Search of an Environmental Ethic." *New Jersey Outdoors* (July–August 1975): 14.
Harper, Robert W. *John Fenwick and Salem County in the Province of West Jersey.* Associated Printers, 1978.
Highlands Nature Friends. "A Brief History." http://www.highlandsnaturefriends.org/history.html.
Hufford, Mary. *One Space, Many Places: Folklife and Land Use in New Jersey's Pinelands National Reserve: Report and Recommendations to the New Jersey Pinelands Commission for Cultural Conservation in the Pinelands National Reserve.* American Folklife Center, Library of Congress, 1986.
Lewis, William J. *New Jersey's Lost Piney Culture.* The History Press, 2021.
Library of Congress. "Bill McKibben Speaks on 'American Earth: Environmental Writing Since Thoreau.'" https://www.loc.gov/item/2021687953.
———. "Public Law 91-516-Oct 30, 1970." https://www.congress.gov/91/statute/STATUTE-84/STATUTE-84-Pg1312.pdf.
Lovell, Percy B. "Under 'The Old Hat' of the Country Editor." *Moorestown Chronicle*, August 3, 1950.
Magnum, Michael. Personal interview with the author. March 22, 2024.
McGarry, Michael. "Teaching Environment LEHT Man to Be Honored." *Press of Atlantic City*, January 31, 1991.
McKibben, Bill, and Al Gore. *American Earth: Environmental Writing Since Thoreau.* Penguin Putnam, 2008.
McPhee, John. *The Pine Barrens.* Noonday Press, Farrar, Straus and Giroux, 1968.
Michalsky, B.V. *Whitesbog: An Historical Sketch.* Conservation and Environmental Studies Center, 1978.
Milken Educator Awards. "Educator Profile: Shaina Brenner." https://www.milkeneducatorawards.org.
Miller, Elaine Ruth. "Walking Lightly on the Planet: A Curriculum Enrichment for the Pinelands Science Unit of the Cherry Hill Environmental Education Residency Program on Pinelands Ecology." Master's thesis, Rowan College of New Jersey, 1995.
Milstead, Harley P. *New Jersey: People, Resources, and Industries of the Garden State.* John C. Winston Company, 1946.

Moonsammy, Rita Zorn, David Steven Cohen and Lorraine E. Williams, eds. *Pinelands Folklife.* Rutgers University Press, 1987.
Moore, Kirk. "Portrait Honors Pines Baroness." *Asbury Park Press*, October 7, 1998.
Moore, Kirk, and Paula Scully. "Pine Barrens Scientist, Educator Dies at 93." *Asbury Park Press*, August 19, 2008.
National Park Service History eLibrary. "Growth of the National Park System, 1964–1972." http://npshistory.com/centennial/0616/timeline.htm.
National Park Service. "New Jersey Pinelands: Basic Information." www.nps.gov.
New Jersey Pinelands Comprehensive Management Plan: Progress Reports on Plan Implementation. Pinelands Commission, 1980.
New York Times. "Robert H. Morrison, a Jersey Educator." March 28. 1973.
Oak 1960 Yearbook. Published by the students of State College Glassboro, New Jersey, 1960.
Ocean County New Jersey. "Pinelands Jetport by C&H Staff." http://www.co.ocean.nj.us/WebContentFiles/e0fcc5ac-2335-4071-8bd7-31d0f2ea9b86.pdf.
Official Site of the State of New Jersey. "Forest Resource Education Center." www.nj.gov.
———. "1970: A State Agency Charged with Protecting the Environment Is Born." https://dep.nj.gov/earthday/timeline/m1970.
O'Leary, Cathy. Personal interview with the author. January 30, 2024.
O'Leary, Terry. *Ecotour Trail Guide to Great Bay Boulevard, Tuckerton Seaport*, 2000.
———. Personal interview with the author. January 10, 2024.
Olsen, Judith Lamb. *Pemberton: An Historic Look at a Village on the Rancocas.* Polyanthos, 1976.
Olsen, Judith M. *Pemberton Township: A History.* Friends of the Pemberton Community Library, 1976.
Online Library of Liberty. "Quote [by Adam Smith]." https://oll.libertyfund.org.
O'Rourke, Shaun. Personal interview with the author. May 31, 2024.
Palumbo, Joe. Personal interview with the author. January 29, 2024.
Patterson, Frank G. *Exploitation of the Pine Barrens, Past, Present and Future.* Conservation and Environmental Science Center, 1969.
Philadelphia Inquirer. "Trying to Save a Piece of History." October 3, 1983.
Pine Barrens Coalition. "The New Jersey Pine Barrens." 1981.
Pine Barrens Native Fruits. "Our History." www.pbnf.co/history.html.
Pinelands Cultural Society. "Remembrances of Gladys Eayre." *Pinelands Cultural Society Newsletter* 29, no. 1 (February 2004).
Pinelands Folklife Project collection (AFC 1991/023). American Folklife Center, Library of Congress.
Pinelands Institute for Natural and Environmental Studies (PINES). "Souvenir of Pinelands Institute for Natural and Environmental Studies Browns Mills, New Jersey." November 21, 1989.
Raabe, Christine. Personal interview with the author. February 29, 2024.
Reddington, Linda, and Karen Sudol. "A Little Piece of Paradise." *Times-Beacon*, October 28, 2000.
Reupert, Andrea, Shulamith Lala Straussner, Bente Weimand and Darryl Maybery. "It Takes a Village to Raise a Child: Understanding and Expanding the Concept of the "Village." *Frontiers in Public Health* 10 (March 2022). doi: 10.3389/fpubh.2022.756066.
Riley, Karen F., and Andrew Gioulis. *Legendary Locals of the Pine Barrens of New Jersey.* Arcadia Publishing, 2013.
Rillo, Thomas J. *Historical and Philosophical Foundations of Outdoor and Environmental Education.* Self-published, 2019.
———. *Not Finished Just Begun.* Self-published, 2016.

Sambolin, Annette. Interview with Dr. Eugene Vivian. New Jersey School of Conservation, February 17, 2008.

———. Interview with Dr. Eugene Vivian. New Jersey School of Conservation, July 26, 2007.

———. *The New Jersey School of Conservation from 1949 to 1999.* D&M Printing, 2005.

Sandler, Ross. "The Refuse Act of 1899: Key to Clean Water." *American Bar Association Journal* 58, no. 5 (May 1972): 468–71.

Scout Patch Auction (blog). "Walter Head Acorn Award Info Circa 1936." October 24, 2012. http://thescoutpatchauction.com.

Sharp, Daisy. "There's More Than Just 'Those Woods' at Whitesbog." *Sun Trenton Times Advertiser*, September 7, 1975.

"A Sharp Education: About L.B. Sharp." https://asharpeducation.weebly.com.

Sinton, John. *Natural and Cultural Resources of the New Jersey Pine Barrens.* Center for Environmental Research, Stockton State College, 1978.

Snyder, David B., and V. Eugene Vivian. *Rare and Endangered Vascular Plant Species in New Jersey.* U.S. Fish and Wildlife Service, 1981.

Sobel, David. *Beyond Ecophobia: Reclaiming the Heart in Nature Education.* Orion Society, 1996.

———. *Place-Based Education: Connecting Classrooms and Communities.* Orion Society, 2004.

State of New Jersey Pinelands Commission. "New Jersey Pinelands Biosphere Region." www.nj.gov/pinelands/reserve/bio.

Stockton University. "Stockton to Host 25th Annual Pinelands Short Course in March 2014." Stockton Pinelands Course 2013 Press Release. https://stockton.edu/news/documents/archive/StocktonPinelandsCourse2013PressRelease.pdf.

Storer, John H. *The Web of Life: A First Book of Ecology.* Devin-Adair, 1953.

Sullivan, Frank E., and William H. Schlesinger. "The Environmental Education Act: Where Do We Stand Now?" *BioScience* 22, no. 6, 1972: (361–63). http://www.jstor.orgstable/1296342.

Suplee, Carol. "The Quietest Force in the State's History." *Burlington County (NJ) Times*, November 6, 1988.

Tiedermann, John. Personal interview with the author. April 17, 2024.

Vinal, William Gould. *Nature Guiding.* Press of W. F. Humphrey, 1926.

———. *Nature Recreation Group Guidance for the Out-of-Doors.* Dover, 1963.

Vivian, V. Eugene. *Sourcebook for Environmental Education.* C.V. Mosby, 1973.

Vosseller, Bob. "'Autumn Adventure' Honors, Remembers Volunteers." *Beacon*, November 27, 2008.

Walker, Tamara. "Meryl Streep, Tim Howard, Kevin Smith Headline 2024 New Jersey Hall of Fame Class." *Asbury Park Press*, July 17, 2024.

Walton, Rae, and Gene Vivian. *The Ancestry Of Vincent Eugene Vivian.* Newton, Massachusetts, 2003.

Washington Post. "1936–1992: History of Olympic Torch Relays." https://www.washingtonpost.com/wp-srv/sports/olympics/longterm/torches/history.htm.

White, Joseph J. *Cranberry Culture.* Orange Judd, 1870. Available at the Internet Archive, https://archive.org.

White, J.P. "Camp to Be Renamed After Environmentalist." *Tuckerton Beacon*, January 20, 2000.

Whitesbog Preservation Trust. "June Mershon Vail, 1922–2012." *Whitesbog Preservation Trust Newsletter* (1st Quarter 2013): 2.

———. "Whitesbog History." https://whitesbog.org/history-about.

Wikipedia. "Elizabeth Coleman White." https://www.wikipedia.org.

———. "List of Defunct Councils (Boy Scouts of America)." https://www.wikipedia.org.
———. "Patriarchy." https://www.wikipedia.org.
Wong, Alia. "The U.S. Teaching Population Is Getting Bigger, and More Female." *The Atlantic*, February 20, 2019.
Woodford, Elizabeth M. "Summer in the New Jersey Pine Barrens." *Horticulture* (July 1968): 29.
Young, George E. "A Resident Environmental Education Program for Pinelands Regional High School: A Handbook for Administrators and Teachers." Thesis for Glassboro State College, May 1990.
Young, George. Personal interview with the author. January 8, 2024.

ABOUT THE AUTHOR

William J. Lewis is a lifetime resident of the New Jersey Pine Barrens, as were multiple generations of his family before him. He is the author of *New Jersey's Lost Piney Culture* (The History Press, 2021), *Adventure with Piney Joe: Exploring the New Jersey Pine Barrens* (South Jersey Culture and History Center, 2022), *South Jersey Legends & Lore: Tales from the Pine Barrens and Beyond* (The History Press, 2024). He shares his Piney adventures on social media networks under the name Piney Tribe. He preaches exploration without exploitation and teaches our children to be tomorrow's environmental stewards. After proudly serving as a U.S. marine, William went on to graduate from Rider University; he founded an environmental nonprofit to get kids outdoors and has served in leadership roles for both government and New Jersey nonprofit organizations.